German Surface Raider Warfare

German Surface Raider Warfare

The Ships and Operations of the German Imperial
Navy During the First World War, 1914-18
ILLUSTRATED

Edited by John Humphrey

LEONAUR

German Surface Raider Warfare
Tthe Ships and Operations of the German Imperial Navy During the First World War,
1914-18
ILLUSTRATED
Edited by John Humphrey

First published under the title
Review of German Cruiser Warfare 1914-1918

Leonaur is an imprint of Oakpast Ltd

ISBN: 978-1-78282-624-8 (hardcover)
ISBN: 978-1-78282-625-5 (softcover)

http://www.leonaur.com

Publisher's Notes

Contents

CHAPTER 1

Summary of Operations

This monograph is a summary of information which may bear on the operations of German surface raiders. It is mainly based on the *German Official History of Cruiser Warfare 1914-18* (*Kreuzerkrieg*, 3 Vols., I.D. Translation) which gives a detailed account of the operations of the Cruiser Squadron, the light cruisers *Emden*, *Koenigsberg* and *Karlsruhe* and the auxiliary cruisers *Kaiser Wilhelm der Grosse*, *Cap Trafalgar*, *Kronprinz Wilhelm*, *Cormoran*, *Prinz Eitel Friedrich*, *Moewe* (two cruises), *Greif*, *Wolf*, *Seeadler* and *Leopard*. The tonnage captured by each vessel, its length of cruise, theatre of operations, etc., are tabulated below.

Name.	Tonnage Captured.	Length of Cruise, Theatre of Operations.	Remarks.
Cruiser Squadron (Von Spee)	1,600	Four months...	Destroyed, Battle of Falklands, 8th December, 1914.
DRESDEN	12,927	Six months ; S. Atlantic and S. Pacific	Destroyed, Juan Fernandez, 14th March, 1915.
LEIPZIG	15,299	Four months ; N. and S. Pacific	Destroyed, Battle of Falklands, 8th December, 1914.
EMDEN	82,938	Nine weeks ; N. Pacific and Indian Ocean	Destroyed off Cocos Island, 9th November, 1914.
KOENIGSBERG	6,600	Indian Ocean. Blockaded in river, end of October, 1914	Finally destroyed 11th July, 1915.
KARLSRUHE	76,609	Three months, N. and S.	Destroyed by internal explosion, 4th November, 1915.
KAISER WILHELM DER GROSSE	10,400	Three weeks, N. Atlantic ...	Destroyed at coaling anchorage, 26th August, 1914.
CAP TRAFALGAR	Nil	Six weeks ; S. Atlantic ...	Destroyed at coaling anchorage, 14th September, 1914.
KRONPRINZ WILHELM...	60,522	Over 8 months ; N. and S. Atlantic	Interned Newport News, 11th April, 1915.
CORMORAN	Nil	Four months ; N. and S. Atlantic	Interned Guam, 14th December, 1914.
PRINZ EITEL FRIEDRICH	33,423	Over 7 months ; N. and S. Pacific and S. Atlantic	Interned, Newport News, 10th March, 1915.
MOEWE (1st Cruise)	57,776	Two months ; N. and S. Atlantic	Returned to Germany, 5th March, 1916.
MOEWE (2nd Cruise)	124,713	Four months ; N. and S. Atlantic	Returned to Germany, 22nd March, 1917.
GREIF	Nil	Two days	Sunk in North Sea, 29th February, 1916.

WOLF	38,688	Fifteen months; N. and S. Atlantic and Pacific (Mines)	Returned to Germany.
	73,988		
SEEADLER	27,923	N. and S. Atlantic and S. Pacific; 7½ months	Wrecked, Mopihaa Island, 2nd August, 1917.
LEOPARD	Nil	Six days	Sunk in North Sea, 16th March, 1917.
Total	623,406	.	

All the above ships except the *Kaiser Wilhelm der Grosse*, *Moewe*, *Wolf, Seeadler, Greif* and *Leopard* were already abroad when hostilities commenced. The first four of these successfully evaded the North Sea—Atlantic blockade, the *Seeadler* having been allowed to proceed after examination. The *Moewe* (twice) and *Wolf* also escaped the patrols on their homeward journeys. The *Greif* and *Leopard* were destroyed before reaching the oceanic routes as a result of special intelligence which may be considered as an exceptional factor of the war. Further information bearing on the operations of the Cruiser Squadron and light cruisers will be found in Chapter 2, and the auxiliary cruisers in Chapter 3. Track charts of each vessel are included.

Fuelling and supply was perhaps the most difficult problem which faced the German raiders and Chapter 4 is devoted to that subject. The activities of all these different types of ships depended on the supply and embarkation of coal and the change over to oil should be taken into consideration before drawing inferences from 1914-18. Oil can be easily transferred on the high seas, but coal cannot, except under particularly favourable conditions. The *Kaiser Wilhelm der Grosse* and *Cap Trafalgar* were soon brought to action because their coaling anchorages were discovered whereas the *Kronprinz Wilhelm* which always coaled in the open sea successfully evaded her pursuers.

Similarly, the immunity of the *Moewe* and *Wolf* may be partly traced to the large coal reserves carried in their own holds. Fuel supply is likely to remain the Achilles heel of raiders in distant waters, though possibly not to the same extent as in 1914-18. Air reconnaissance is another factor which may influence operations. Few ships carried aircraft in the First World War, but the *Wolf*'s seaplane proved of great value. Wireless communications have also developed during the years following the war, but they exercised an important influence on the raiding operations of 1914-18, and Chapter 5 has, therefore, been devoted to "Intelligence and Communications."

The German raiders captured 623,406 tons of shipping (including 74,000 sunk by the *Wolf*'s mines). The lion's share of 454,712 tons went to the *Moewe, Wolf, Emden* and *Karlsruhe*. They inflicted very heavy losses on British shipping although the heavier submarine sinkings tended to obscure the fact. In addition, they held up trade and transport for long periods besides immobilising a very large number of allied cruisers in distant waters. Under the circumstances, it seems extraordinary that they were not used on a larger scale. The following remarks in the *German Official History* bear on this point:—

The *Moewe* and *Wolf* only appeared in the third year of the war. The submarine had already achieved considerable success by then and was more economical of time and personnel in comparison with tonnage sunk. The auxiliary cruiser did, however, supplement the war on commerce by operating in distant waters which were not threatened by submarines.

A larger number of auxiliary cruisers of the *Moewe-Wolf* type would not by themselves have won the war, but in conjunction with submarines, might in the years 1917-18 have been able to contribute what was wanting to secure victory, particularly if the North and South Atlantic routes had been seriously threatened at their terminals. Auxiliary cruisers would, however, have been particularly valuable at the *commencement of the war* had they been employed at once in large numbers.

If for instance, the colliers of the supply bases at Manila and Batavia had each been fitted at Kiaochow with a single gun and a supplementary active service crew commanded by efficient young commanders—then, at a time, when no merchant ships had been armed, the trade in Australian and Indian waters would have been completely disorganised. The effect of these auxiliary cruisers might have been greatly strengthened by the *Emden*, perhaps also the *Nuremberg* in the Far East, and by the *Dresden* and *Leipzig* on the West Coast of South America. Owing, however, to everything being subordinated to the battle fleet and by systematic opposition to the *jeune école*, cruiser warfare on a *grand* scale had never been thoroughly considered. Nevertheless, the weaker naval power possesses a powerful weapon in the auxiliary cruiser, which has greater effect, if wielded energetically, at the outbreak of war simultaneously in all oceans.

The measures adopted against raiders are referred to in greater detail in Chapters 2 and 3. Prior to the war, the Admiralty adopted the principle that the surest way of affording protection to trade was to make a prompt attack on the enemy's fighting ships, the destruction of which was stated to be the primary object in maritime war. The Atlantic Ocean was divided into zones designated by letters, to each of which a cruiser force was allocated. The idea seems to have been that they should concentrate their efforts in the focal and terminal areas, but in practice, operations against raiders mainly consisted of searching areas and anchorages in which they were thought to be working.

In some cases, shipping was diverted from the normal routes and also temporarily held up in harbour. For example, all sailings from Aden and Bay of Bengal ports were stopped when the *Koenigsberg* and *Emden* appeared in these areas. Similarly, troop transports were detained in certain harbours following reports of the *Moewe* (2nd cruise) and *Wolf*. The provision of escorts for transports was another measure. For example, they were enforced in the Indian Ocean on the 4th March, 1917, on account of the *Wolf*, discontinued on 2nd June and re-introduced in December, following an out-of-date report from the Maldive Islands. These were not convoys in the ordinary sense of the word for a single cruiser often escorted only one or two transports. No attempt was made to include cargo ships although this might have been arranged.

Viewed through the perspective of the years, it must be admitted that these counter-measures did not afford much protection to shipping or attain a high degree of success in destroying the actual raiders. During 1916 and 1917, we maintained abroad, exclusive of the Mediterranean, an average of 6 old battleships, 35 cruisers, 13 large auxiliary cruisers and 9 destroyers besides a large number of sloops. In addition, the French had 4 cruisers on the oceanic routes and the Japanese lent 8 cruisers and 4 destroyers, making a grand total of 6 battleships, 47 cruisers, 13 auxiliary cruisers and 17 destroyers. This large force performed various useful duties but its main function was to protect trade and hunt down raiders.

Only three of the latter were at work during these two years, the *Moewe* for six months, the *Wolf* for twelve, and the *Seeadler* for seven-and-a-half, but there is very little evidence that they were seriously hampered by the measures taken against them. Exclusive of the ships of the German Cruiser Squadron, a total of 12 raiders operated on the oceanic routes at different periods of the war. One was sunk by internal explosion, three were interned, three returned to Germany and one was wrecked. Four were destroyed in battle, but of these the *Kaiser Wilhelm der Grosse* and *Koenigsberg* cannot be entirely credited to our strategical dispositions for the breakdown of the German supply organisation played an important part in their destruction.

Again, the *Emden's* fate depended on a lucky chance and the policy of patrolling and searching was only fully justified in the case of the *Cap Trafalgar*. It nearly succeeded when the *Suffolk* surprised the *Karlsruhe* in the West Indies, but the actual result was to drive her into a more remunerative area. Similarly, when things became too hot for her on the normal South American trade route, she withdrew by chance on to the diverted track and made several captures.

It appears that our cruisers in distant waters would have been more effectively employed in convoying trade, especially as the Allies had more than sufficient for the purpose. This policy would have greatly reduced the sinkings besides cutting off the raiders' source of fuel supply from captured vessels. Even if convoy had been confined to ships carrying coal, the activities of the *Emden, Karlsruhe, Prinz Eitel Friedrich, Kronprinz Wilhelm, Moewe* and *Wolf* would very soon have been brought to a dead stop.

During the last year of the war, arrangements were made for introducing a world-wide convoy organisation at short notice but, by that time, raiding operations had ceased. Also, early in 1918, plans were worked out for convoying the Atlantic trade with battleships to guard against possible raids by German battle cruisers and an American battle squadron was stationed at Berehaven for that purpose.

CARMANIA SINKING THE GERMAN ARMED LINER "CAP TRINIDAD" OFF TRINIDAD SEP 14. 1914. THE FIRST NAVAL ENGAGEMENT BETWEEN ARMED LINERS.

CHAPTER 2

German Cruiser Squadron and Light Cruisers

GERMAN CRUISER SQUADRON.

It is unnecessary to say much about the movements of this squadron. They are described in the Naval Staff Monographs, but the German History contains some additional information. When Admiral Von Spee decided to leave the China Seas and make for the West Coast of South America, he realised that that course of action would provide few opportunities of damaging British shipping. The question of taking the Squadron into the Indian Ocean was considered, but rejected owing to the difficulty of maintaining coal supplies. On despatching the *Emden* into that area he made the following entry in his war diary:—

A single light cruiser, which consumes far less coal and can, if necessary, coal from captured steamships, will be able to maintain herself longer than the whole Squadron in the Indian Ocean, and as there are great prizes to be won there (Indian, East Asiatic and Australian shipping), it seems advisable to despatch our fastest light cruiser, the *Emden*, with our best collier. She can subsequently proceed to the African coast, or should Holland remain neutral, to the Netherland East Indies.

Commenting on the operations which led up to Coronel, the *German History* says:—

The operations of the Allies were undoubtedly severely hampered by the fact that they were not directed from the outset towards seeking out and engaging our Main Force. Their oper-

13

ations against German intelligence centres and bases in the Pacific soon developed into expeditions for territorial conquest, so that some of their naval forces were diverted from their main objective for a considerable time. They must soon have become aware, however, that the German ships were not remaining in close proximity to German bases and colonies. The operations against the Cruiser Squadron were hampered further by the necessity for protecting the transport of numerous troops, who were urgently needed owing to the situation in the European theatre of war. These smaller operations interfered with the systematic co-operation of the East Asiatic and Australian forces.

In addition, the British Naval History indicates that the plan conceived in peace time to combine the China, Australian and East Indies Squadrons to form an Eastern Fleet under the Commander-in-Chief, China Squadron, was not carried out completely in 1914, but that the Commander-in-Chief and the Commander-in-Chief, Australia, worked side by side under direct orders from the Admiralty, and that the Admiralty, here and in other theatres of war, restricted the Admirals' freedom by concerning themselves with details.

It is evident also that the Admiralty were sometimes unable to obtain concurrence with their strategic views and were repeatedly obliged to give way to the local interests of the Australian and New Zealand Governments. The Australian Navy Board, in particular, appears to have been allowed a certain independence as regards strategic decisions.

At times, one commander-in-chief, did not even know what the other was doing; in the first particularly critical period they did not even remain in wireless telegraphy communication, although, with energetic co-operation, they might quite possibly have found the German Squadron and engaged it. After the entry of Japan into the war, the co-operation of the Allies still remained faulty, although they received many indications of Graf von Spee's whereabouts and destination; this want of co-operation was chiefly due to the pursuit of local objectives and the lack of close cohesion of the forces under one command. The strategic position which brought disaster to the British at the Battle of Coronel was the outcome of these defects.

The plan of keeping two forces, one on the east and one on the west coast, each strong enough to engage the Cruiser Squadron, was undoubtedly right, given the possibility of doing so with the ships available. It was necessary that each force should be considerably superior to the Cruiser Squadron, the fighting efficiency of which was known; it was also necessary to have a number of fast ships available, so that when the enemy had been found they could keep in touch with him until the Main Body came up.

If the forces available were inadequate for this purpose, it would undoubtedly have been advisable to concentrate the Main Force at the Falkland Islands, detaching a few fast cruisers to watch that part of the coast where the Cruiser Squadron would probably pass; this was Admiral Jerram's original plan and Admiral Cradock no doubt had it in mind when he proposed to assemble his forces at the Falkland Islands.

After the Battle of Coronel, the Naval Staff advised Von Spee to try to break through with all his ships and return to Germany, and that was his intention on leaving Valparaiso. The idea of attacking the Falkland Islands at the very commencement of the homeward journey brought about the destruction of his ships at the guns of Sturdee's Squadron. There can be little doubt that that battle and the destruction of the *Emden* off Cocos Islands will tend to make German raiders in foreign waters avoid attacks of a military nature, and confine themselves strictly to commerce warfare. Even before the event, the officers of the Squadron were by no means unanimous on this question. The captains of the *Gneisenau*, *Leipzig* and *Dresden* thought it strategically unsound to approach the Falkland Islands. The *History*, whilst admitting that a successful landing would have weakened the British position, remarks:—

> The damage to the enemy would however, be of a temporary nature only, because the Cruiser Squadron would be unable to hold the base for any length of time. It was in no way necessary in the interests of future operations to attack the Falkland Islands, and as the British wireless telegraph stations would certainly send out warning signals before they were destroyed, the whereabouts of the Cruiser Squadron would be disclosed, thus lessening the chances of breaking through for home. The chance of surprising the enemy shipping off the La Plata would also be forfeited, though it was very important both as regards damaging the enemy and procuring coal for the Squadron.

Further, if enemy forces were encountered, even a successful action would result in exhausting the German supplies of ammunition long before fresh supplies could be sent from home and might also result in damage to ships and engines.

In a discussion on the general principles of cruiser warfare against trade, the German historian lays down that a commander should as far as possible avoid action with hostile forces and that this rule becomes even more binding when bases for effecting repairs are not available. It is stated that a cruiser captain must in such circumstances avoid all acts likely to assist the enemy in locating him. Such acts include attacks on shore establishments except when undertaken for some very special purpose.

The *History* also criticises the passivity of the High Sea Fleet at the time of the Falklands Battle and seems to suggest that the action of forces in distant waters can be synchronised with those at home to the mutual advantage of both. It says:—

> The early end of the Cruiser Squadron prevented the High Sea Fleet from co-operating with it, but it would be false to assume that there was no possibility of such co-operation, especially if the war had been of short duration. The operations carried out at a great distance from home waters had affected British strategy, to an enormous degree and the continuance in the Atlantic of those operations might well have caused such distribution and movements of the Grand Fleet as to afford the High Sea Fleet opportunities for obtaining military successes, and thus exercising a direct and decisive influence on the war.
>
> Special emphasis must, however, be laid on the fact that, if the High Sea Fleet had taken energetic action in the North Sea during the months October-December, 1914, the British would have found it difficult if not impossible, to detach ships to operate against the Cruiser Squadron. This Squadron might then have achieved further military successes, which would not have failed in their effect on the situation in home waters. Finally, if the Cruiser Squadron had executed the operation of breaking through into the North Sea in co-operation with the High Sea Fleet, an action between the British and German Fleets might have ensued and the results might have been decisive for the whole war.

The Cruiser Squadron did not meet any merchant shipping in its passage across the Pacific, but the auxiliary ship *Titania* captured the *Helicon* (1,600 tons) and the *Leipzig*, the *Valentine* (3,150 tons) and *Drummuir* (1,844 tons), all loaded with coal, off the South American Coast. The capture of the *Drummuir* turned out to be an unfortunate incident for the Germans. She was intercepted to the eastward of Cape Horn on the 2nd December and towed to Picton Island where her cargo was transferred to the supply ships *Baden* and *Saint Isabel*. This delayed the Squadron's arrival at the Falkland Islands by three days but as she sank beneath the waves no one knew that her capture had sealed her captor's fate.

Very little need be said about the *Leipzig's* movements before joining the Pacific Squadron. She was in Mexican waters on the outbreak of war and after cruising as far North as San Francisco, proceeded to Easter Island, capturing the two British ships *Elsinore* and *Bankfield en route*. She sank two more ships in company with Von Spee's Squadron which brought her total captures up to 15,299 tons.

The *Dresden* proceeded from the West Indies to the East Coast of South America with the intention of attacking trade to the southward of the River Plate, sinking two British ships, the *Hyades* and *Holmwood* on the way. But her engines needed refitting and an anchorage in Orange Bay near Cape Horn was chosen for that purpose. Whilst carrying out this work, the *Dresden* was ordered to the West Coast and after joining the Cruiser Squadron sank two more ships which brought her total captures up to 12,927 tons.

The *Dresden* was the only German cruiser to escape from the Battle of the Falklands. At first two battle-cruisers and ten cruisers were employed in searching for her, but after about a fortnight this was reduced to four cruisers and one auxiliary cruiser. Nevertheless, she remained at large for over three months. The numerous bays and inlets of Tierra del Fuego provided excellent hiding places, but the *Dresden* frequently communicated with Punta Arenas by motor boat, etc., and she would probably have been quickly located if the intelligence organisation, centred in London and Monte Video over 1,200 miles away, had not proved defective.

Despite this handicap, the British Vice-Consul (unpaid) at Punta Arenas, who had his own business to attend to, did obtain accurate information of the *Dresden's* hiding places on two occasions. His first telegram does not seem to have reached the Admiralty which had become convinced that she was hiding in an almost inaccessible fjord, Last Hope Inlet, an idea which appears to have been spread by the

Germans themselves. Orders were issued from London to search it, and the *Kent* was despatched to Valparaiso to obtain the necessary charts. The Admiralty did not know that the captain of the *Glasgow* had arranged with the English Manager of a local company to report the arrival of any ship in that district and before his telegram, to that effect, reached London, further instructions were issued. The *Bristol* was now ordered down from Monte Video and she and the *Glasgow* proceeded to Union Sound *en route* for Last Hope to await the return of the *Kent*.

This move left the southern coast clear for the *Dresden* and she proceeded into the Pacific on the 14th February. Five days later, the vice-consul learnt that she had been seen at the southern end of the Barbara Channel but the *Glasgow* was now in Last Hope Inlet, where the *Bristol* had seriously damaged her rudder by striking a rock. After his return, the captain of the *Glasgow* arranged for a search of the southern area, but on 3rd March the Admiralty informed him that the *Dresden* had now been definitely located in Last Hope Inlet. He realised that his own ship had probably been mistaken for the German Cruiser but the Admiralty was not easily convinced and ordered the *Glasgow*, *Bristol* and *Orama* to proceed once again on a hopeless quest to the Last Hope labyrinth.

In the meantime, the *Kent* was following a more reliable clue obtained from an intercepted signal ordering the German collier *Gotha* to rendezvous in 37° S. and 80° W., about 200 miles south of Mas-a-fuera. On 7th March, the *Kent* sighted the *Dresden* in that position, but she had not the necessary speed to catch her and the only ship that had, was bottled up in Last Hope until slack water on the following day. The *Kent* did, however, intercept an important signal from the *Dresden* which on being deciphered pointed to a rendezvous at Juan Fernandez, where the *Dresden* was brought to action and destroyed on 14th March.

EMDEN. (Plate I.)

The *Emden* was a comparatively modern light cruiser, displacing 3,650 tons, mounting ten 4.1-inch guns with a speed of 24 knots. Her movements, including names, etc., of ships sunk, are shown on the accompanying track chart (Plate I); the anchorages she used will be found in the Appendix, and some details of her fuelling arrangements in Chapter 4.

She captured 82,398 tons of British shipping in less than six weeks,

THE NOTORIOUS GERMAN CRUISER "EMDEN" SUNK BY H.M.A.S. "SYDNEY" OFF COCOS ISLAND. 9TH NOVEMBER, 1914.

besides seriously dislocating trade in the Indian Ocean. She also destroyed the Russian light cruiser *Zhemchug* and the French destroyer *Mousquet*, fired the Madras oil tanks and interrupted communications with Australia by cutting the cable at Cocos Islands. Another important effect of the *Emden's* operations was to delay the transport of British troops from India and Australia. The *History* also infers that the *Emden's* appearance in the Indian Ocean had considerable effect on the native population, although insufficient to have any material influence on the movement for the overthrow of British rule.

It is stated that numerous disaffected Indians returned to their native land from America and Japan on the outbreak of war. Apparently, they were supplied with arms and money but the rapidity with which Germany was cut off from overseas countries, prevented anything but isolated outbreaks which were quite uncoordinated and without lasting effect. An attempt to convey a large quantity of arms from North America to India in the steamship *Maverick*, failed owing to what is termed "the one-sided neutrality of the United States."

The captain of the *Emden's* report contains various hints on the best methods of effecting a capture. He recommends that the ensign should not be shown until the ship to be boarded is only a short distance off and that the signals "Stop" and "Do not use your wireless" should be hoisted at the same time. Searchlights should be used as little as possible and the cruiser kept in a position relative to the prize in which the latter cannot ram her.

A considerable increase in the complement of cruisers engaged in such work is recommended so that armed guards, or prize crews for colliers, can be formed. The additional ratings should as far as possible be reservists from the Mercantile Marine and should include engineers and stokers. Officers of the Reserve are invaluable for the command of captured colliers or armed guards, particularly those who have experience of the area in which the cruiser is operating.

Prizes were usually sunk by opening the Kingston valves, removing the doors of condensers and opening up the ballast pump valve chests. Openings in bulkheads were made by explosive charges during the night or by shell fire during day light. It was found that vessels sunk more rapidly if holed either forward or aft, but not at both ends.

In view of the necessity for keeping secret the area in which a cruiser is operating, the disposal of the crews of captured vessels is stated to be important. In certain cases, their landing must be delayed as long as possible, and if a vessel with sufficient accommodation and

S.M.S. Emden BEACHED

provisions for numerous passengers and crews is available, the problem can be solved by keeping her in company for the necessary time. The enemy can then be prevented from receiving early news of the cruiser's position, her methods, supply bases, and use of auxiliary vessels, etc. Nevertheless, a neutral merchant ship fitted with wireless will, as a rule, disclose the cruiser's position to any enemy warship she may meet and in any case the disclosure is bound to occur on her arrival in port. The absence of reports from ships due at certain signal stations and non-arrival at their destinations will also enable a cruiser's area of operations to be inferred. Delay in landing crews will, therefore, only be of real value in keeping a cruiser's operations secret, when no neutral vessels have been stopped or when her position is such that signal stations or ports will only be reached after a lengthy voyage.

The German historian states that the *Emden's* operations in the Indian Ocean will stand as a model of cruiser warfare against commerce and remarks that:—

> Captain Von Mueller delivered his blows where they would have the greatest political and economic effect. His sudden appearance and disappearance at the scene of operations and a correct appreciation of the enemy's counter moves enabled him not only to achieve success in each individual operation, but also to render his capture difficult. It was not luck, but the capacity for forming an accurate estimate of the situation from the scanty information obtainable from prizes and intercepted wireless, that were responsible for his achievements in spite of all the enemy's endeavours to catch him. Far from keeping to any fixed scheme, Captain Von Muller instantly dropped a predetermined course of action when circumstances rendered a change of plan desirable.

The naval measures taken to deal with the *Emden's* attack on trade consisted in employing numerous cruisers in searching anchorages and areas in which she had been reported or was suspected of operating. The number varied but on the average totalled 1 battlecruiser (Japanese), 4 armoured cruisers, 4 cruisers, and 2 auxiliary cruisers. In addition, there were 2 Russian cruisers in the Indian Ocean. Some of these cruisers were slower than the *Emden* so that even if they had located her, she would probably have escaped like the *Karlsruhe* did. In any case, frequent changes in the theatre of operations usually rendered the intelligence, on which they acted, misleading or out-of-

H.M.A.S. SYDNEY

date. This system did not effectually protect the trade or succeed in bringing the *Emden* to action. Her eventual destruction was due to a lucky chance that the *Sydney*, escorting troop transports from Australia, happened to be in the vicinity when she raided the Cocos Islands.

If the attack had been timed a few hours earlier or later she might have escaped. There can be little doubt that convoy on the principal trade routes in the Indian Ocean would have greatly reduced the losses and deprived the *Emden* of coal from captured colliers on which she largely depended. It is true that convoy would have slowed up the normal flow of trade but not to the extent that actually happened. Uncertainty as to the *Emden*'s movements led to shipping being held up for long periods in Bombay, Calcutta, Aden and Singapore, so that trade was seriously dislocated throughout the Middle and Far East.

KOENIGSBERG. (Plate I.)

The *Koenigsberg* which was slightly smaller and rather slower than the *Emden*, arrived on the East African Station in June, 1914. She was ordered to leave German East Africa in the event of strained relations and be ready to attack shipping in the gulf of Aden. Her movements are shown on the accompanying track chart (Plate I), and the anchorages she used are tabulated in the Appendix. In addition to ten 4.1-inch guns, the *Koenigsberg* carried a surplus armament of two 22-pr. L/30 guns which together with some smaller guns from the surveying ship *Moewe* were intended for equipping an auxiliary cruiser. Her operations were brought rapidly to an end from lack of fuel.

When the *Koenigsberg* left Dar-es-Salaam on the 31st July, 1914, she passed close to the *Hyacinth*, *Astrea* and *Pegasus* of the Cape Squadron just as it was getting dusk but they failed to keep touch owing to her superior speed. They did however, prevent the collier *Koenig* leaving Dar-es-Salaam and this handicapped the subsequent movements of the *Koenigsberg*, especially as arrangements for obtaining coal from Portuguese East Africa broke down owing to its purchase by the British naval authorities and the restrictions placed on cable messages. The *Koenigsberg*'s attempts to obtain coal by capture in the Gulf of Aden also failed because British shipping was held up or diverted on the outbreak of war.

The *German History* considers that this was due to her excessive use of wireless in warning German ships of the outbreak of war and trying to get in touch with colliers. In any case, the *Koenigsberg* only captured one ship, the *City of Winchester* (6,600 tons) and having burnt

S.M.S. KOENIGSBERG

nearly all her coal made for Ras Hafun on the African Coast where she had to depend on a small supply in the old auxiliary vessel *Somali*. The *German History* states that:—

> The difficulties of cruiser warfare in the northwestern part of the Indian Ocean were enormously enhanced by the monsoon, which in this region blows with gale force from July to September and which not only makes boarding and examination of vessels, the transfer of stores and other operations impossible on many occasions, but also increases fuel consumption whilst reducing considerably opportunities for coaling. These conditions should have been taken into consideration when the mobilisation orders for the East Africa Stations were being worked out.

Lack of fuel decided the captain of the *Koenigsberg* to leave the vicinity of Aden and make for Madagascar on the 23rd August with the intention of attacking French shipping. Arrangements were also made to rendezvous with the *Somali* on arrival in that area. It was realised that a move in the direction of South Africa would have provided better prospects but there was not sufficient coal to get there. Failure to obtain fuel at Madagascar led the cruiser back to the Rufiji River in German East Africa where small quantities were available.

Although the *Koenigsberg* achieved only one actual capture, she seriously disturbed British trade and shipping by her presence in the Gulf of Aden, by the attack on the *Pegasus* at Zanzibar and by weeks of uncertainty as to her whereabouts during September and October, 1914. Her eventual blockade in the Rufiji Delta also immobilised a considerable number of vessels at a time when British naval resources were being strained to the utmost.

The measures to deal with the *Koenigsberg* consisted of searching and patrolling a very large area off the East Coast of Africa. For example, the light cruisers *Chatham*, *Dartmouth* and *Weymouth* were exclusively employed on this duty for over a month, searching as far south as the Angochi Islands about 700 miles from the Rufiji River where the *Koenigsberg* was hiding. It is characteristic of such operations that reports of her movements were nearly always false. The *Pegasus* had already visited that locality but the creeks were believed to be too shallow for the *Koenigsberg*. The search might have continued indefinitely if papers had not been discovered in the supply ship, *Praesident*, indicating that coal had been sent there. The *Koenigsberg* was eventu-

S.M.S. Koenigsberg scuttled

ally blockaded and destroyed in July, 1915. It was lack of coal that brought her activities to an end and limited her achievements to the sinking of H.M.S. *Pegasus* and the *City of Winchester.*

It may be noted that the division of the Western Indian Ocean into two commands tended to complicate the campaign against the *Koenigsberg.* Cooperation between the ships of the East Indies and Cape Stations depended on the issue of orders by the Admiralty, a procedure which was fruitful in delays and misunderstandings.

KARLSRUHE. (Plates II and III.)

The *Karlsruhe* was one of Germany's most modern light cruisers, being rather larger and faster than the *Emden* and *Konigsberg.* During the period of strained relations, she awaited events at an out of the way anchorage, Cay Sal Bank in the Florida Straits. Her subsequent movements, including ships sunk, are shown in Plates II and III. The *Karlsruhe's* first task was to arrange a rendezvous for the conversion of the *Kronprinz Wilhelm* into an auxiliary cruiser. The two ships met in the open sea to the eastward of the Bahamas and at once went alongside each other to transfer guns, stores and men.

The operation was hardly completed, when on 6th August Admiral Cradock's Flagship, the *Suffolk* appeared on the scene and the *Karlsruhe* at once made off to the northward. She had no difficulty in escaping but her coal was running short and the chase drove her further from her supply ships. Captain Kohler therefore, decided to steer for Newport News to coal but the light cruiser *Bristol* was sighted in the moonlight at 8.30 p.m. and barred his way to the North. An ineffective engagement followed at long range but the *Karlsruhe* by altering course to the southward, soon left the *Bristol* behind. The British cruisers were not fast enough to bring the *Karlsruhe* to action but they had depleted her bunkers by steaming at high speed and placed her in an awkward position.

Captain Kohler tried to get in touch with the supply ship *Neckar* during the night but failed and then decided to steer for St. Thomas in the Virgin Islands where the Hamburg-Amerika line maintained a stock of coal. Next day it was ascertained that there was insufficient coal to reach St. Thomas and course had to be altered for San Juan de Porto Rico which was rather nearer. It was estimated that she would arrive there with only 4 tons in her bunkers. The American authorities offered no objection to the *Karlsruhe* coaling at San Juan, but only 800 tons were available, and much of it was dust. Fear of being overtaken by superior forces caused the *Karlsruhe* to leave San Juan the same evening before her bunkers were half full with the intention of filling up at the Dutch Island of Curacoa.

After leaving Curacoa, Captain Kohler decided to make for the North-East Coast of Brazil which promised to be a less dangerous and more profitable area of operations. After picking up the supply ship *Patagonia*, the two proceeded in company, coaling *en route* at Maraca Island, Saint Joao and Lavadeira Reef on the North Coast of Brazil.

The *Karlsruhe* worked with great success off the coast of Brazil from the 30th August to the 26th October (see Plate III). She usually cruised with one or two supply ships disposed in a wide formation across the trade routes and experienced no difficulty in obtaining coal. In addition to German supplies, the *Strathroy* was captured with 5,600 tons on the 31st August, the *Indrani* with 6,700 tons on the 16th September and the *Farn* with 4,400 tons on the 5th October, all three being retained as auxiliaries. During this period, the *Karlsruhe* always coaled off Lavadeira Reef (five times) which she considered the only suitable anchorage in that area.

Captain Kohler realised the danger of overdoing his success and on the 24th October decided to leave the Coast of Brazil and return to the West Indies. He feared that his anchorage would be discovered when the *Crefeld* arrived at Teneriffe with captured crews on the 22nd October and that the *Karlsruhe's* movements would be reported by neutral ships, several of which had recently been intercepted.

After leaving the Pernambuco area, the *Karlsruhe* made what was perhaps her most valuable capture, namely, the *Vandyck* of over 10,000 tons, but the journey to the West Indies was never completed. Her activities ended on the 4th November, when an internal explosion sent her to the bottom. In three months, she had sunk 16 British ships and 1 Dutch, totalling over 76,000 gross tons, and probably caused the British naval authorities as much anxiety as the *Emden*. They did not even have the satisfaction of knowing that she had blown up and continued their efforts to find her for several months.

The measures taken to deal with the *Karlsruhe* consisted of searching suspected anchorages and areas where she was thought to be operating. The actual forces engaged varied, but a total of more than 26 different cruisers and auxiliary cruisers were employed in the search for this particular raider at various times. At the end of August, for example, 12 cruisers and 3 auxiliaries were scouring the West Indies and South American waters for her. In addition to the cruisers which

29

the *Karlsruhe* locked up in the South, an extensive search was made for her in the vicinity of the Azores and Canary Islands in the middle of October about 2,000 miles from her actual position.

Again, on the 23rd October, the *Karlsruhe* was definitely reported to be at anchor in the Bissagos Islands on the West African Coast although she was about 2,500 miles away. Two British and two French cruisers steamed hundreds of miles to search the locality. Six weeks after the *Karlsruhe* had blown up, the battlecruiser *Princess Royal* joined the cruisers in the West Indies in an intensive effort to find the raider and even as late as February and March reports were coming in concerning her movements.

The *German Official History* suggests that the *Karlsruhe* was responsible for the failure to reinforce Admiral Cradock prior to Coronel. It points out that when the powerful armoured cruiser *Defence* arrived at Pernambuco on the 25th October she was sent to relieve the *Cornwall* as guardship at Abrolhos Rock in order that the latter might join other cruisers in a search off the Brazilian coast by which time the raider had left for the West Indies. But whatever opinion may be held on this point, the measures taken neither protected shipping nor succeeded in destroying the raider.

CHAPTER 3

Auxiliary Cruisers

KAISER WILHELM DER GROSSE. (Plate XIII.)

The *Kaiser Wilhelm der Grosse*, a fast liner of 22,700 tons gross, was commissioned at Bremerhaven on 2nd August with an armament of six 4.1 -inch and two 1.45-inch guns. She sailed on 4th August and her subsequent track is shown on Plate XIII. The captain intended to pass between Iceland and the Faroes but British wireless signals seemed to indicate that that area was being watched and he decided to break out to the northward of Iceland. He had been informed that Las Palmas supply base would distribute 15,000 tons of coal in colliers on position lines off the Azores, Canary Islands and Cape Verde, but no collier was found on the rendezvous line to the northward of the Azores and it was decided to make for the Rio de Oro (Durnford Point, West Africa).

The British steamer, *Kaipara* 7,392 tons gross, and the *Nyanga*, 3,066 tons gross, were captured in the vicinity of the Canary Islands. Both were sunk and the crews taken on board. The British mail steamers, *Galician*, 6,762 tons gross, and the *Arlanza*, 15,044 tons gross, were also stopped and examined, but allowed to proceed owing to the difficulty of accommodating their crews and passengers.

The German collier, *Duala*, was met on the Canary Island rendezvous line on 15th August and directed to Rio de Oro, but she had only 800 tons of coal on board. After anchoring in Rio de Oro Roads on 17th August, the *Kaiser Wilhelm der Grosse* proceeded to sea again to search the rendezvous line for another collier as by that time the *Duala* had only 500 tons left. She failed to find it and returned to Rio de Oro to coal. But a large liner consumes a lot of fuel when steam has to be maintained, and by the time the *Duala* was cleared on 20th August, she only had 1,221 tons on board, whereas 2,500 were required

Kaiser Wilhelm der Grosse sunk by H.M.S. *Highflyer*

to reach her prospective operating area off the South American Coast.

The Las Palmas base had made liberal provision for coal, but the *Slawentzitz* with 5,000 tons had been captured and the *Walhalla* with 2,000 tons was taken by the *Kronprinz Wilhelm*. The *Magdeburg* arrived at Rio de Oro on the 24th August with 1,400 tons, the *Arucas* with 1,500 and the *Bethania* with 6,000 on the 25th. The *Kaiser Wilhelm der Grosse* at once commenced coaling and by noon on the 26th had 2,100 tons on board. Coaling was still proceeding when the *Highflyer* appeared on the scene at 12.30 p.m., and after a short engagement the *Kaiser Wilhelm der Grosse* was scuttled by her own crew. She had sunk 10,400 tons of shipping.

The destruction of this raider was brought about by her having to wait for coal supplies at Rio de Oro for over a week, and, if the German account is correct, the delay was partly due to the action of the British Consul in preventing the full loading of the *Duala*. The *Kaiser Wilhelm's* position became known through a passenger from Rio de Oro, informing the British Consul at Las Palmas on 24th August that she had anchored there on the morning of 17th August. H.M.S. *Highflyer* happened to call at Las Palmas just as the news came in and she proceeded to investigate with the result stated above.

CAP TRAFALGAR. (Plate XIV.)

The *Cap Trafalgar*, a fast liner of 23,300 tons gross, was requisitioned by the German Naval Attaché at Buenos Aires on 15th August for service as an auxiliary cruiser. Her movements are shown on Plate XIV. An attempt to complete with coal, water and provisions at that port failed owing to the unfriendly attitude of the Argentine authorities. She then proceeded to Monte Video and after coaling sailed for Trinidada Island. There she met the *Eber* which had arrived from German S.W. Africa and after transferring the gunboat's two 4.1-inch and six 1.46-inch guns and crew, the *Cap Trafalgar* was commissioned on 31st August.

There were two German and one American colliers at Trinidada, but coaling was difficult owing to the heavy swell, and after taking in 600 tons it was decided to proceed to Rocas Rock. After completing with coal there, the captain of the *Cap Trafalgar* intended to steam South accompanied by colliers and operate off the River Plate area. He steered towards Rocas from the 4th to 9th September, and then decided to return to Trinidada Island. It appeared from intercepted wireless messages that the British cruisers *Cornwall, Bristol, Berwick*

THE GERMAN ARMED LINER "CAP TRAFALGAR" SUNK BY H.M.S. "CARMANIA" AFTER A MOST EVEN ENGAGEMENT WHICH LASTED 1 HOUR 45 MINUTES. OFF TRINIDAD, SOUTH ATLANTIC, SEPT 14, 1914.

and *Monmouth* were in the vicinity, and it was considered inadvisable to continue the journey any further to the northward. Also, a wireless message from the *Karlsruhe* indicated that she would require the colliers at Rocas.

The *Cap Trafalgar* anchored off Trinidada for the second time on 13th September. The captain at first intended to leave at once with the colliers. The anchorage no longer seemed safe to him as the *Eber* must have already arrived at Bahia to be interned. However, there was very little swell at the time and he decided to fill up with coal as rapidly as possible and leave not later than the following afternoon. It was a fatal decision. During the forenoon of the 14th, a strange ship was sighted which afterwards proved to be the British auxiliary cruiser *Carmania*. The *Cap Trafalgar* at once stopped coaling, weighed anchor and raised steam in all boilers.

In the subsequent action, the much heavier armament of the *Carmania* soon silenced the *Cap Trafalgar*'s guns and after receiving several hits near the waterline she commenced to heel over and sink. The *Carmania* also suffered a great deal of damage principally from a fire in the superstructure, and had to be escorted to Gibraltar for repairs. On meeting the *Cap Trafalgar*, she was on her way South to patrol the Monte Video area and had been ordered by Admiral Cradock to inspect Trinidada Island, *en route*, with the above fortunate result.

KRONPRINZ WILHELM. (Plate IV.)

The *Kronprinz Wilhelm* was a fast liner of 22,700 gross tons which arrived at New York at the end of July, 1914. A few reserve officers joined her on the afternoon of 3rd August and that evening she sailed, in accordance with instructions, for a rendezvous to the eastward of the Bahamas. Her conversion to an auxiliary cruiser took place alongside the *Karlsruhe* on the high seas when the latter transferred two 3.46-inch guns, one machine gun, ammunition and rifles, a number of ratings and her navigating officer, who took over command of the *Kronprinz Wilhelm*. The work was scarcely finished when the *Suffolk* chased the *Karlsruhe* off to the northward. The *Kronprinz Wilhelm* then proceeded to the vicinity of the Azores where she met the German collier *Walhalla* on the rendezvous line and commenced coaling in the open sea. On this occasion, the work continued for three days, after which she proceeded to the southward again.

It is unnecessary to describe the *Kronprinz Wilhelm*'s subsequent movements for they are shown on Plate IV, which includes a list of

S.M.S. Kronprinz Wilhelm

captured ships. Her enormous coal consumption made that type of ship unsuitable for raiding operations in distant waters. All sorts of difficulties were, however, successfully overcome and the risk of capture diminished by coaling in the open sea, steaming slowly ahead, often in a considerable swell. The *Kronprinz Wilhelm* remained under way for over eight months or 250 days without anchoring, 72 of these being spent in coaling or taking in provisions. German supply ships from South American ports supplied some of her needs but the greater part of the coal came from eight captured prizes.

Of 31 ships met during this time, 19 were stopped and 15, totalling over 60,000 gross tons, captured as prizes; 10 steamships and four sailing ships were sunk and one steamer used for the evacuation of captured crews. The cruise ended with her arrival at Hampton Roads on 11th April, 1915, where she was interned. The decision to make for a neutral port was necessitated by the state of the ship which was leaking like a sieve owing to damage received whilst coaling; her boilers and engines were also urgently in need of repair and *beri-beri* had attacked some of the ship's company.

The naval measures directed against the *Kronprinz Wilhelm* consisted of searching anchorages and areas in which she was thought to be operating. She was reported time after time by neutral ships and the fact that most of her captures were made in a comparatively small area of about 500 by 750 miles, in the vicinity of Fernando Noronha, illustrates the difficulty of locating raiders in the ocean spaces. As is usual in such cases, there were many false reports. For example, she was reported to have visited Rio de Oro on the West African Coast and the *Carnarvon* and *Highflyer* were sent to search that area about the middle of September.

CORMORAN.

On 6th August, 1914, the light cruiser *Emden* captured the S.S. *Rjasan* (5,200 tons) of the Russian Volunteer Fleet and brought her into Tsingtao. She was renamed *Cormoran* and commissioned as an auxiliary cruiser by officers and men of the gunboats *Cormoran*, *Iltis* and *Vaterland*. After mounting eight 4.1-inch guns and two searchlights and embarking 2,000 tons of coal, she sailed on 10th August to join the Cruiser Squadron. On arrival at Majuro Atoll on 28th August, Admiral Von Spee gave her and the *Prinz Eitel Friedrich* orders to attack trade on the West Coast of Australia. They had only one collier between them, and after she was cleared the *Cormoran's* activities were

S.M.S. CORMORAN

severely limited by the necessity of finding more coal. The supply bases in Far Eastern Waters had sent out a larger number of colliers but, by the time the *Cormoran* had returned to the Dutch East Indies, many of them had been driven out of Dutch ports and captured.

The idea of attacking trade off Western Australia had to be abandoned. After cruising about in search of colliers with several narrow escapes from British and Japanese cruisers, the *Cormoran* entered the American port of Guam on 14th December, where she was interned. She was forced to this course of action by failure to obtain coal which was partly due to the time wasted in meeting the Cruiser Squadron at Majuro Atoll. The *Official German History* commenting on this says:—

> The fault lay, not with the auxiliary cruiser, nor with the supply bases, but was due to the delay of the Cruiser Squadron in recognising the value and purpose of auxiliary cruisers.

PRINZ EITEL FRIEDRICH. (Plate V.)

The liner *Prinz Eitel Friedrich* (16,000 tons gross) arrived at Tsingtao on 2nd August, 1914, where she was converted into an auxiliary cruiser by the officers and men of the gunboats *Luchs* and *Tiger*. Stores, four 4.1-inch and six 3.46inch guns were quickly transferred and after coaling she left to join the Cruiser Squadron at Pagan Island. On sailing from Majuro Atoll for South America, Admiral Von Spee detached the *Prinz Eitel* and *Cormoran* to attack trade on the West Coast of Australia, but lack of coal prevented them getting there.

The *Prinz Eitel*, however, was luckier than the *Cormoran* in obtaining 2,000 tons at Malakal Harbour in the Pelew Islands. She then decided to make for South America and rejoined the Cruiser Squadron at Mas-a-Fuera on 27th October. Her subsequent movements and ships captured are shown on Plate V. The *Prinz Eitel* was left on the West Coast when Von Spee sailed for the Falkland Islands and she remained there until the middle of January. During that time, three allied ships of over 9,000 gross tons, including the French sailing ship *Jean* with 3,000 tons of Welsh coal, were captured.

After coaling from the *Jean* at Easter Island, it was decided to make for Germany *via* Cape Horn, but the East Coast of South America proved a profitable area and the idea of returning home faded into the background. Between 26th January, 1915, and 20th February, the *Prinz Eitel* sank eight allied ships of about 24,000 tons, but none of them were able to supply her with coal which was urgently required. On 24th February, there were only 1,000 tons remaining in the bun-

S.M.S. Prinz Eittel Friedrich

kers or less than half the amount required to take her home. The engines and boilers were also in need of repair and it was decided to proceed to Chesapeake Bay where she was interned on 10th March, 1915. The depredations of the *Prinz Eitel Friedrich* were thus brought to an end by lack of fuel. The lucky capture of the *Jean* probably saved her from internment on the West Coast, and cost the Allies 24,000 tons of shipping.

MOEWE—First Cruise. (Plates VI and VII.)

Ocean liners with a large coal consumption were in most respects unsuitable for raiding operations in distant waters and the fitting out of the *Moewe* at the end of December, 1915, marked the recognition of that fact. The idea emanated from proposals forwarded by Lieutenant Theodor Wolff (reserve), who wrote:—

> As a fast liner converted to an auxiliary cruiser has too large a coal consumption it would be preferable to fit out a steamer whose coal consumption was so small and stowage so large that she could go privateering for months without outside assistance . . . . it should not be very difficult for an auxiliary cruiser of the kind to run the blockade. She would put to sea, ostensibly as a cargo steamer escorted by a submarine.

The *Moewe* (about 5,000 tons gross) was originally a banana carrier with a maximum speed of 14 knots. Her armament consisted of four 5.9-inch L/45 and one 4.1-inch L/45 guns and two above water 19.7-inch torpedo tubes. She also carried 500 mines, the laying of which was defined as her first and principal task. Like most instructions given to German captains, those issued to the *Moewe* allowed full scope to his initiative and independent judgment.

The following five minelaying areas were suggested but the choice was left entirely to him:—

No. 1.—To the westward of the Orkneys, off the western exit to the Pentland Firth and Scapa Flow as far as Cape Wrath.

No. 2.—The North Minch.

No. 3.—Off Lough Swilly between 7° and 9° W. and 54° 50' and 56° N.

No. 4.—Off Bantry Bay.

No. 5.—Area off the mouths of the Loire and Gironde inside the 110 fathom line.

S.M.S. Moewe

The *Moewe* left the Elbe on 29th December, 1915, disguised as a Swedish steamer and with a submarine stationed 40 miles ahead to escort her out of the North Sea. Her subsequent track and names of ships sunk are shown on Plates VI and VII. Half her complement of mines was laid to the westward of the Orkneys on the night of 2nd January, 1916, and it was on this minefield (the Whiten Bank field) that the battleship *King Edward VII* was sunk a few days later. The remainder were laid on 9th January, 1916, off the Gironde in the Bay of Biscay.

The choice of area for attack on shipping was left to the captain, but attention was directed to the importance of war material from Canada and the U.S.A. and grain supplies from the Argentine. The desirability of sending back to Germany prizes with important supplies was strongly emphasised. The second ship captured by the *Moewe* was the British, *Corbridge* with nearly 5,000 tons of coal. A prize crew was placed on board and she was ordered to make for a rendezvous near the estuary of the Amazon. The *Moewe* then continued her cruise and after capturing several more ships coaled from the *Corbridge* off the Maraca Islands (North Coast of Brazil), the name and position of the anchorage being carefully hidden from the crew and prisoners.

On 15th February, in the vicinity of the Cape Verde Islands, the captain decided to make for home. He considered that sufficiency of coal could always be found but that the engines required a thorough overhaul. The ships captured during this cruise included four with cargoes of coal but only one was used, the remainder being sunk.

The *Moewe* passed into the North Sea about 100 miles South of Iceland and sighted a number of British warships off the southwest corner of Norway. The captain stated that they were not stopping neutral ships and that the discovery of the *Moewe* would have been inevitable if they had. She arrived home on 5th March, 1916, the cruise having lasted just over two months during which time she captured 57,776 tons of shipping. The *Moewe* changed her appearance four times with paint and sheet iron panelling, disguising herself as a P. & O. liner, an Argentine transport, one of the Hall Line and finally as the Swedish steamer *Bia*.

MOEWE—Second Cruise. (Plates VIII and IX.)

The *Moewe* left Kiel for the second time on 22nd November, 1916, disguising herself as the Swedish steamer *Marie Sverigi* before passing through the Little Belt. Three submarines were to have escorted her out of the North Sea, but owing to bad weather, the captain decided to press on without them. The *Moewe* passed between Iceland and the Faroes, after inferring from intercepted wireless messages that two auxiliary cruisers of the Iceland-Faroes patrol were meeting each other at 8.0 a.m. on 27th November in Lat. 62° to 63° N. and Long. 12° to 13° W. She crossed that area about midnight.

It is important to note that on this occasion the Allies received early notice of the *Moewe's* activities from the Belgian Relief Ship *Samland*, which was stopped and examined on 4th December. Her wireless was destroyed but she gave the alarm on arrival at Falmouth three days later. Our naval forces in the North and South Atlantic were therefore warned that a raider had broken out and every effort was made to intercept her. This cruise may, therefore, be viewed as a test of the measures adopted against raiders at that stage of the war.

The movements of the *Moewe* and her list of captured ships are shown on Plates VIII and IX. The *Yarrowdale* which was intercepted on 11th December had a valuable cargo of war material and was sent back to Germany with a prize crew. The *Saint Theodore*, captured on 12th December with 7,000 tons of coal, was utilised as an auxiliary cruiser and armed with two guns taken from captured ships. She was renamed the *Geier* and after parting company, did not meet again until 16th January when the *Moewe* embarked 1,700 tons of coal from her in mid-Atlantic.

After arranging various rendezvous, the *Geier* was sent off to operate on the sailing ship route between Cape Horn and Europe, "in so far as this may be possible without interference with your chief duty as collier." They met again on 11th February at Trinidada Island where the *Moewe* coaled once more. By this time, the *Geier's* engines and boilers were in a bad state of repair and she was sunk with explosive charges on 14th February. She had sunk two sailing ships of about 1,500 tons.

The *Moewe* narrowly escaped destruction on 9th January when she captured the *Minieh* and as this incident may provide some useful lessons it will be described in detail. The light cruiser *Amethyst* when patrolling about 150 miles to the eastward of Pernambuco had stationed her collier, the *Minieh*, 20 miles ahead with orders to report any suspicious vessels by wireless. She increased speed during the morning and sighted the *Minieh* about 8 miles distant, three points on the starboard bow and then dropped back out of sight.

Just before dark, smoke was observed from the direction of the collier's assumed position but suspicion was not aroused as no signals were received. It was ascertained afterwards that a vessel had approached the *Minieh* from ahead during the late afternoon, but the Captain did nothing because he "only had orders to report suspicious vessels." At 5.0 p.m., when the steamer was only half a mile away, she hoisted the German ensign, trained out her guns and made a signal to stop using wireless. The captain of the *Minieh* stated he told the wireless operator to disregard that order and to signal "What ship is that" and make the S.O.S. According to the *British Official History*, Vol. IV, nothing was heard in the *Amethyst's* wireless room. In any case, the *Minieh* was sunk almost in sight of the *Amethyst* after the crew and confidential documents had been removed.

The evidence of the *German History* is probably more reliable than that of the *Minieh's* captain and the *Amethyst's* wireless ratings both of whom were under suspicion of neglect of duty. According to it, the *Minieh* did commence to signal but at the first letter the *Moewe* "jammed with high energy and. fired a warning shot." The *German History* also states that the *Minieh's* captain was semi-intoxicated which seems possible in view of his failure to report the *Moewe* sooner.

One of the questions arising out of this affair is the importance of jammed W/T signals as indications of attacks on shipping. All the German raiders made a routine of jamming their victims' calls for help and sometimes this occurred in comparatively close proximity to British cruisers. It looks as if the latter's wireless operators were only interested in decipherable messages and did not realise that signs of jamming might be of great practical importance. Certainly, with directional apparatus, they may provide a definite clue to the position of a hostile raider.

It is also important to note that this was one of the few occasions on which a German raider narrowly escaped destruction in the ocean spaces as the result of a prearranged plan. Most of the narrow escapes described in the *British Official History*, such as when the *Emden* passed within 100 miles of the slow battleship *Triumph* cannot be accurately described as such. In any case, this incident raises the question whether the numerous cruisers searching for raiders might not have had more success by using merchant ships as decoys and following them through dangerous areas at a prearranged distance.

Another point is whether it would not have been expedient and more in accordance with the principles of international law to appoint a commissioned officer to a collier used in this manner as an auxiliary. The German raiders frequently followed that routine with

S.M.S. Moewe SUNK

regard to prizes and supply ships, by placing one of their own officers temporarily in command, assisted by a few ratings. If that procedure had been followed in the case of the *Minieh*, it is improbable that the *Moewe* would have escaped. Nor would she have been able to obtain valuable information concerning British dispositions from confidential documents which the *Minieh's* captain neglected to destroy.

Another interesting case which occurred during this cruise was that of the *Otaki* (9,500 tons gross) in ballast from London to New York, armed with one 4.7-inch gun. The *Moewe* sighted her on 10th March but owing to the violent movements of the raider which was steaming head to sea and the difficulty of gun-laying, she closed to 2,400 yards before making the signal to stop. As the *Otaki* refused to do so, a brisk action ensued in which the *Moewe* fired 35 rounds of 5.9-inch, 23 of 4.1-inch and three torpedoes. Although the *Otaki* was soon overpowered she scored three hits which did a great deal of damage by flooding a compartment and starting a fire in the coal bunkers. According to the *Moewe's* report, the situation became very serious more especially as the ammunition was only separated from the burning coal by a wooden partition. Two days of the most strenuous exertions were required to extinguish the fire and avert the danger.

Amongst the numerous British armed merchantmen captured by German raiders, the *Otaki* is the only one that succeeded in damaging her opponent, and this was probably due to the exceptionally short range at which the action took place. At ordinary ranges, it was practically impossible, for merchant ships to score a hit quickly because they were not supplied with rangefinders which would have made all the difference in these encounters. The *Moewe* had already commenced the homeward journey before meeting the *Otaki*, and her second cruise ended at Kiel on 22nd March. In four months, she had sunk 19 steam and five sailing ships, totalling 119,600 tons gross.

The naval measures directed against the *Moewe* are not the least instructive part of the story. On the *Samland's* report reaching the Admiralty, troopships in various localities were retained in harbour and very strong naval forces directed to search for her. Approximately 24 British cruisers and auxiliary cruisers and an unspecified number of French were employed patrolling different routes and areas in the North and South Atlantic. Despite the expenditure of an enormous amount of fuel and energy, the *Moewe* continued to sink ship after ship on the principal trade routes. One single armed merchantman defied the power of the combined navies because of the fundamental dif-

S.M.S. Grief

ficulty of locating ships on the wide expanse of the ocean. There can now be little doubt that if the Atlantic trade had been organised into convoys and escorted by the numerous cruisers that were scouring the sea, these heavy losses would have been prevented.

GREIF.

After the departure of the *Moewe* on her first cruise, the German merchant ship *Guben* (4,963 gross tons) was fitted out as an auxiliary cruiser. She was renamed the *Greif* and armed with four 5.9-inch guns and two broadside torpedo tubes. Her task was defined as attack on commerce. The choice of the theatre of operations was left to the captain's discretion but particular attention was directed towards the shipment of war material from North America and wheat from the River Plate, the export of which commences in February.

The *Greif*, disguised as the Norwegian steamer *Rena*, left the Elbe on the evening of 27th February, 1916, submarine U.70 being stationed 40 miles ahead with orders to turn back in about Lat. 59° 20' N. On 28th February, the Admiralty received information that a raider had left Germany and special arrangements were made to intercept her by auxiliary cruisers of the Northern Patrol and five light cruisers and seven destroyers dispatched from Scapa and Rosyth.

About 9.0 a.m. on 29th February, the *Alcantara* and *Andes* sighted a steamer about 70 miles to the northeastward of the Shetlands. It was the *Greif* and as the *Alcantara* was lowering a boat to examine her the raider hoisted the German ensign, dropped her screens and opened fire. A fierce action ensued during which two torpedoes, fired at the *Alcantara* missed. With only one serviceable gun left, the raider fired a third torpedo which sank the *Alcantara*. But the *Andes* and *Comus* had now arrived on the scene and soon reduced the *Greif* to a blazing wreck.

WOLF. (Plates X, XI and XII.)

The German merchant ship *Wactfels* of 5,809 gross tons and 10.5 knots, was requisitioned for conversion into an auxiliary cruiser in March, 1916. She was renamed *Wolf* and armed with seven 5.9-inch guns and four torpedo tubes. The work was completed by the end of May, but her departure was postponed until November owing to the short summer nights which greatly increased the chances of interception by the British patrols. The operation orders (*Kreuzer Krieg*, Vol. 3, p 239) issued by the Naval Staff are summarised below:—

Departure at your own discretion. High Sea Fleet provides sub-

H.M.S. ANDES

marines for reconnaissance and screening duties; S.M.S. *Wolf* is to arrange independently with the latter. If strong enemy counter-action is experienced or may, from observation, be anticipated, it is left to your discretion to postpone the enterprise until a more favourable period.

Task.—The approaches to the most important ports of British India and British South Africa, as well as the inter-connecting trade routes, are to be contaminated with mines. The chief ports are: Colombo, Bombay, Karachi, Calcutta, Rangoon, Singapore, Cape Town—the last-named port is to be mined *first* and, in addition, at least five ports in such sequence as may seem fit to the captain. An entirely unexpected appearance in the area of operations is essential for the success of the task; everything must, therefore, be avoided on the outward journey which may lead to the presence of the auxiliary cruiser *Wolf* being suspected.

In allocating the mines to the various harbours and trade routes, it should be borne in mind that it is more advantageous to mine a large number of places with a few mines, than a few places with a large number of mines.

The minefields must be laid irregularly so as to render their clearance more difficult. Their depth-setting must be so regulated—having regard to tidal current and range of tide—that their presence shall not be prematurely betrayed by medium-sized steamers running on to them.

After execution of the mining tasks, war on commerce is to be pursued until all resources are exhausted. The choice of operation area is left to your own judgment. Main objective for attack is the grain trade from Australia to Europe, which continues throughout the year.

In order to keep the presence of the *Wolf* secret as long as possible, it is desirable that only such ships shall be stopped whose destruction is legitimately permissible.

Resources.—Support from home or from neutral countries abroad must not be relied on.

It is desirable that a suitable prize vessel shall be utilised to accommodate the passengers from other prizes. Neutral countries will not grant an asylum to German prizes. Prizes that are to be sent to a neutral port must, therefore, previously (in accordance with paragraph 114 of the Prize Regulations) be employed as

H.M.S. Alcantara in action

auxiliary ships and must also have been converted into warships in accordance with the "Agreement concerning the Conversion of Merchant Ships into Warships."

The auxiliary war vessel hoists ensign and pendant; the captain, who must be an officer shown in the Navy List, on the active list or in the reserves, receives a written appointment; the crew is detailed from the crew of the auxiliary cruiser, but may be augmented from any native personnel that may be found on board the prize; the prize must be armed. The conversion may not take place in neutral waters.

These prize vessels, converted into auxiliary warships, must not carry on independent war on commerce.

If prizes converted into auxiliary cruisers, and armed, are to be employed for cruiser warfare the greatest care is to be observed that the terms laid down in the VIIIth Hague Convention are fulfilled.

When war on commerce offers no more prospects of success and an attempt to return home seems inexpedient, the ship is to be laid up.

Special care is to be observed to prevent our enemies from learning that we are able to read their ciphered messages.

The *Wolf* left Kiel on 30th November after embarking 465 mines, 6,285 tons of coal and one seaplane. She was escorted through the North Sea by three submarines disposed about 40 miles ahead. A fourth, U.66 proceeded in company, being towed part of the way submerged and connected by telephone. The subsequent track of the *Wolf* is shown on Plates X, XI and XII. The ship steamed through a vast icefield which had made a particularly early appearance in the Denmark Straits but a full moon enabled the ship to escape damage.

Only one ship was sighted *en route* to the Cape where the first minefield was laid on the night of 16th January. The war diary of that day remarks:—

In order that the best possible results may be achieved, the mines must be so placed that the full extent of the minefield shall not be revealed on the first ship striking mines. The location of its position must be rendered as difficult as possible, as also its clearance or avoidance. Location and clearance become the easier the more numerous the mines laid at the harbour entrance and the closer they lie together. Avoidance is rendered

S.M.S. Wolf

more difficult by a greater extension of the minefields. Further, the movements of the *Wolf* when executing this task, if observed at all, must arouse no suspicion. She must not, therefore, steer too conspicuous courses. The order enjoins that the mines shall only be effective against large ships. Accordingly, the line Dassen Island to Slang Kop Point in about 40 to 50 fathoms of water, will be best for the mined area; and the mines must be distributed as indicated in the sketch map by shaded rectangles.

Detailed plans of the minefields laid off Cape Town, Cape Agulhas, Colombo, Cape Comerin, Bombay, Bass Straits, North of New Zealand, Cook Strait, and Singapore are given in the *German Official History* (Vol. 3). The laying of these minefields was usually a slow business. Positions had to be accurately fixed, careful soundings taken, in some cases illumination by searchlights had to be avoided and delays also occurred due to passing steamers.

The detailed description of work conveys the impression that the *Wolf* would have been detected if patrols had been maintained off Cape Town, Colombo and Bombay by harbour craft or even small motor boats. It had also been intended to lay mines off Karachi but an intercepted wireless signal, indicating the discovery of the Bombay minefield, led to a change of plan. Karachi had probably been forewarned and it was decided to proceed to the southward with the intention of attacking trade and obtaining coal.

The British ship *Turritella* was captured on 28th February and commissioned as an auxiliary cruiser under the name of *Iltis* with an armament of one 2-inch gun and 25 mines. She was instructed to proceed to the Straits of Perim and mine the main channel between the Red Sea and Gulf of Aden. The *Wolf* also obtained from her the route prescribed for British shipping between Colombo and Aden. Other cases might be mentioned in which failure to destroy confidential documents provided German raiders with valuable information. Another British ship, the *Jumna*, was captured on 2nd March, and 247 tons of coal from her bunkers were transferred at sea.

On 8th March, the captain of the *Wolf* correctly inferred the recapture of the *Iltis* from an intercepted wireless message describing the *Wolf* and her aeroplane. But part of it was already out of date for the *Wolf* had been repainted.

During the next three months or so, the *Wolf's* movements were mainly governed by the problem of replenishing her coal supply, but no ships were sighted on the Colombo-Aden or Cape-Colombo routes and it was decided to make for New Zealand. Only one ship, the *Dee*, in ballast, was captured on the sailing ship route from Australia between 12th March and 2nd June, despite frequent air reconnaissance. The utmost economy in coal had to be exercised and the monotony of the voyage began to tell on officers and men.

After being continuously at sea for six months, the *Wolf* anchored at Sunday Island in the Kermadecs on 27th May in order to carry out a thorough overhaul of engines and boilers. A cargo ship was sighted passing the Island on 2nd June, but the *Wolf* could not raise steam in time to intercept her. The seaplane was sent up instead and after dropping a message underlined with a bomb conducted the prize to the anchorage. She was the *Wairuno* with a general cargo and 1,150 tons of bunker coal.

This lucky capture dispelled the gloom which had settled on the raider's crew and another steamer with 500 tons of coal was seized on 6th August, thanks to intercepted wireless messages reporting her time of arrival, etc., at Rabaul. The coal could not be transferred at sea and this was done at Offak Harbour (Waigen Island) after the seaplane had examined the anchorage.

Having replenished her coal supply, the *Wolf* proceeded to lay three minefields, the first off the Northwest corner of New Zealand, the second near Cook Straits and the third in the Bass Straits. The last of these tasks was completed on the night of 3rd July, and it was decided to lay the remaining 110 mines near Singapore. The *Wolf's* report states that on the way there, a British cruiser of the Talbot class was sighted near the Karaminta Straits. It was a bright moonlight night and the situation seemed so critical that the *Wolf* nearly altered course to get within torpedo range but apparently, her presence was not detected.

The last batch of mines was laid on the Singapore-Hong Kong and Saigon-Manila routes on 4th September, and the *Wolf* then made for the Indian Ocean to renew the attack on shipping. Nothing was sighted until 26th September, when the Japanese steamer, *Hitachi Maru* with a general cargo and 1,150 tons of bunker coal was captured in the One and Half Degree Channel. The coal and part of the cargo were transferred to the *Wolf* at the Suadiva Atoll (Maldives) and Cargados Carajos (East of Madagascar).

The captain of the *Wolf* now intended to make for home *via* the Cape and to reach the Denmark Straits before the middle of December, 1917, but the capture of the Spanish steamer *Igotz Mendi* on

10th November, with 5,580 tons of coal, led to a prolongation of the cruise. After transferring 900 tons at Cargados Carajos, she was commissioned as an auxiliary and the two ships separated, having first arranged various rendezvous.

They met again near Trinidada Island (S. Atlantic) on the 19th December with the intention of coaling there, but an intercepted wireless message indicated that the island was under military control. The two ships thereupon proceeded some 600 miles to the southward in search of smooth water, but the *Igotz Mendi* seemed to roll in even the calmest sea. Only 550 tons were embarked and both ships seriously damaged in the process.

On 10th and 11th January, the *Wolf* again went alongside near the Equator. This time she embarked 515 tons but frames and bulkheads were buckled and serious leaks developed. On the way home, the *Wolf* experienced very bad weather in the North Atlantic and the leaking vessel nearly foundered. However, she reached German waters safely on 17th February, 1917, though the *Igotz Mendi* ran ashore on the Skaw in a fog and became a total wreck.

The voyage of the *Wolf* had lasted nearly 15 months. During that time, she captured 14 ships of 38,688 tons, all of which, except the *Igotz Mendi*, were sunk. In addition, 13 ships totalling 73,988 tons were lost on her minefields and five ships of 34,587 tons damaged and towed into harbour. Thus the total tonnage captured and sunk by mines amounted to 112,398 tons. Details of the losses on the different minefields are tabulated below:—

1. Minefield, Cape Town ; laid 16th January, 1917.

Date of Striking Mine.	Name.	Nationality.	Gross Tonnage.	Result of Mining.
26.1.17	Matheran	English	7,654	Sunk.
12.2.17	Cilicia	English	3,750	Sunk.
26.5.17	C. de Eizaguirre	Spanish	4,376	Sunk.
10.8.17	City of Athens	English	5,604	Sunk.

2. Minefield, Cape Agulhas ; laid 18th January, 1917.

Date of Striking Mine.	Name.	Nationality.	Gross Tonnage.	Result of Mining.
6.2.17	Tyndareus	English	11,000	Damaged, brought in.
26.8.17	Bhamo	English	5,244	Damaged, brought in.

3. Minefield, Colombo; laid 15th February, 1917.

Date of Striking Mine.	Name.	Nationality.	Gross Tonnage.	Result of Mining.
17.2.17	WORCESTERSHIRE	English	7,175	Sunk.
21.2.17	PERSEUS	English	6,728	Sunk.

4. Minefield, Bombay; laid 19th February, 1917.

Date of Striking Mine.	Name.	Nationality.	Gross Tonnage.	Result of Mining.
11.617.	CITY OF EXETER	English	9,373	Damaged, brought in.
16.6.17	UNKSU MARU	Japanese ...	2,143	Sunk.
24.6.17	MONGOLIA	English	9,505	Sunk.
29.7.17	OKHLA	English	5,288	Sunk.
17.11.17	CROXTETH HALL	English	5,872	Sunk.

5. Minefield, Aden; laid by ILTIS, 4th March, 1917.

Date of Striking Mine.	Name.	Nationality.	Gross Tonnage.	Result of Mining.
20.3.17	DANUBIAN	English	5,064	Damaged, brought in.
5.1.18	HONG MOH	English	3,910	Damaged, brought in.

6. Minefield, Cape Maria van Diemen, N.W. corner of New Zealand; laid 25th June, 1917.

Date of Striking Mine.	Name.	Nationality.	Gross Tonnage.	Result of Mining.
26.6.18	WIMMERA	English	3,622	Sunk.

7. Minefield, Bass Strait; laid 3rd July, 1917.

Date of Striking Mine.	Name.	Nationality.	Gross Tonnage.	Result of Mining.
6.7.17	CUMBERLAND	English	9,471	Sunk.

8. Minefield, Cook Strait; laid 27th June, 1917.

Date of Striking Mine.	Name.	Nationality.	Gross Tonnage.	Result of Mining.
18.9.17	PORT KEMBLA	English	4,700	Sunk.

9. Minefield, Anamba Islands, near Singapore; laid 4th September, 1917.
No ship ran foul of this barrage. It was laid too deep, in error.

Before ending these comments on the *Wolf*, it is necessary to refer back to the *Iltis* (ex-*Turritella*). She reports sighting H.M.S. *Fox* in the Gulf of Aden but was not stopped. On the night of 4th March, her mines were laid in the pre-arranged position. All but one had been dropped when she was challenged by a darkened vessel. A protracted exchange of signals followed but the name *Turritella* seemed to arouse suspicion. When it became apparent that the patrol ship was determined to examine the *Iltis*, the sea-cocks of the latter were opened and explosive charges fired. According to the German account, the sloop *Odin*, the patrol vessel in question, had an old Lloyd's register which did not include the *Turritella* and except for this, she would have been allowed to proceed.

With regard to the measures adopted against the *Wolf*, they were similar to those employed against other raiders. Although the first definite information concerning her was not received until 5th March, the Cape, East Indies and China Stations had been warned to prepare for raiders early in January after the *Moewe* was known to be out. At that time, there were 16 British cruisers, nine sloops and six destroyers in these areas, besides three French and four Japanese cruisers and four destroyers. During the next two or three months, these were reinforced by three British and five Japanese cruisers and four destroyers, making a total of 31 cruisers, 14 destroyers, and nine sloops, etc.

When news of the *Turritella* first came in, the Admiralty stopped all transports in the Indian Ocean, ordered those *en route* to Colombo to be met and escorted, and later issued instructions that transports proceeding to the Persian Gulf and East Africa must be escorted. At the end of March, eight cruisers were convoying transports in the Indian Ocean though in most cases, escorting only one or two ships. The remainder were patrolling various areas and searching localities, without any reliable guide to the *Wolf's* position.

On 2nd June, 1917, it was decided to cancel escorts in the Indian Ocean because no raider had been reported for several months. Accordingly, when the *Wolf* entered the Indian Ocean again early in September, transports in that area were unprotected. Similarly, in December, 1917, when the *Wolf* was thousands of miles away in the Atlantic, escorts were reintroduced because her visit to the Maldive Islands in September had just been discovered.

SEEADLER. (Plate XV.)

The idea of using a sailing ship as a raider emanated from Sub.

S.M.S. SEEDLER

Lieut. Kling, a reserve officer. At first, the idea was not favourably received by the Naval Staff, but personal representations carried the day and he was authorised to select a suitable vessel. The choice fell on a full rigged ship *Pass of Balmaha* of 1,571 gross tons, which had been captured by U.36. She was renamed *Seeadler*, fitted with a 1,000-H.P. motor and two 4.1-inch guns, the latter being hidden under a cargo of timber. She sailed from Germany on 21st December, 1916 disguised as the Norwegian ship, *Hero*.

Great pains were taken to conceal her true character and a search was even made for Norwegian-speaking German seamen. An armed merchant cruiser, the *Patia* of the 10th Cruiser Squadron, stopped the raider between Iceland and the Faroes on Christmas Day, but the boarding officer found nothing suspicious and she was allowed to proceed. It is very difficult to examine a vessel thoroughly without unloading her cargo and at first sight it may seem that such mistakes are unavoidable. It had, however, been suggested to the Trade Division of the Naval Staff early in 1916 that as Lloyd's Register contained the exact dimensions of merchant ships, including such details as dimensions of cylinders, etc., the disguise of ships passing under false names could be penetrated by careful examination.

The subsequent track of the *Seeadler* and the ships captured by her are shown on Plate XV. It will be noticed that she operated for over two months in an area about 360 miles long and 180 miles wide to the northwestward of St. Paul's Rock, capturing nine ships and taking 260 prisoners. The latter were transferred to the French barque *Cambronne* on 21st March and their arrival at Rio de Janeiro on 30th March was the first definite information of the *Seeadler's* activities. But she was already well on her way towards Cape Horn with the intention of filling up with drinking water at one of the sheltered anchorages *en route*.

On the night of 16th April, an intercepted wireless message from Port Stanley indicated that the route round Cape Horn was being watched by British cruisers, and it was decided not to anchor but to attack the sailing ship route in the Pacific after giving Cape Horn a wide berth.

Towards the end of July, signs of *beri-beri* appeared amongst the ship's company and the *Seeadler* arrived off the uninhabited Island of Mopihaa (Society Islands) on the 31st of that month with the intention of obtaining fresh food. As the channel was too shallow to enter the lagoon, she anchored outside, close to the reef and sheltered from the prevailing easterly winds. On 2nd August, the wind suddenly shifted to the westward, whilst some of the ship's company were on their way ashore, and the *Seeadler*, dragging her anchor, was soon crashing on the coral. Despite every effort to get her off she became a total wreck. The cruise had lasted 7½ months, during which time she captured 27,923 tons of shipping.

With regard to the measures taken to deal with the *Seeadler*, the *Lancaster* and auxiliary cruisers *Orbita* and *Otranto* were ordered from the West Coast of South America to the vicinity of Cape Horn on 1st April and the *Avoca* from Esquimalt to search the Galapagos Islands on 28th April. The disadvantages of controlling operations in distant waters from the Admiralty were discernible in these dispositions. Not only did they clash with instructions issued by the senior officer on the spot but the *Otranto* and *Orbita* were kept off Cape Horn against his judgment long after the *Seeadler* had passed into the Pacific. He considered that the chances of intercepting her in that area were small, owing to the long winter nights and that the real danger lay on the important trade route to the northward of Valparaiso which was left unprotected.

LEOPARD.

After the *Wolf*, *Moewe* and *Seeadler* had successfully evaded the blockade it was decided in 1917 to fit out one of the *Moewe*'s prizes, the *Yarrowdale* (4,652 tons gross) as a raider. She was renamed *Leopard* and armed with five 5.9-inch guns, four 3.4-inch and two torpedo tubes. Her operation orders issued by the Naval Staff contained a great deal of detailed information concerning the numbers, movements and dispositions of the Northern Patrol, acquired from intercepted wireless messages.

At that stage of the war, the Germans and ourselves were getting very valuable intelligence from each other's signals but neither seems to have fully realised that this two-edged weapon was being used against themselves. It looks as if Intelligence and Operations were working in watertight compartments. The former must have understood the importance of reducing wireless signals to the minimum whilst the latter was keeping its opponent's intercepting stations working at high pressure.

The German deciphering station stated on 7th March that the patrols between Scotland and Greenland had been strongly reinforced since the beginning of that month. This was communicated to the *Leopard*, but her captain replied that despite the augmented patrols he

S.M.S. Seedler

accepted responsibility for the success of the enterprise. Whilst passing through the Little Belt on 10th March, he was informed by wireless that the English cipher key had been changed and was urgently recommended to postpone the break through if conditions were considered unpromising. To this he replied:

"Have received telegram. Long live the Emperor."

It is rather extraordinary that whilst the Germans were deciphering our signals and had received so many practical examples of the fact that we were doing the same to theirs, they should have broadcast a message of this sort by wireless. As an organisation grows in size, it is easy to create new departments. The difficulty is to make them co-operate intelligently.

On 16th March, the armoured cruiser *Achilles* and the boarding vessel *Dundee*, whilst patrolling between Scotland and Norway, sighted a ship in Lat. 64° 50' N., Long. 0° 32' E. She was ordered to stop and the captain of the *Dundee*, Commander S. M. Day, R.N.R., lowered a boat to examine her. He regarded her with suspicion and very wisely kept his ship, which was only armed with two 4-inch guns, close up on her weather quarter ready to open fire at a moment's notice. After the boat had been alongside about an hour, the *Leopard* disclosed her identity by lowering the gun screens with a crash. But the *Dundee* was much too quick for her and poured in a deadly raking fire at close range.

The *Leopard* then put her helm over and discharged a torpedo which missed. After firing over 40 rounds and sustaining no damage, the *Dundee* cleared the range for the *Achilles*. The *Leopard* sank after a gallant fight against very heavy odds, and the *Dundee's* boat's crew, who had recognised the dangerous nature of their task, went down heroically with her. The fact that the *Dundee* engaged the much bigger and more heavily armed *Leopard*, inflicting heavy damage without suffering herself reflects great credit on the tactical skill of her captain.

H.M.S. Achilles.

CHAPTER 4

Fuelling and Supply

The organisation for supplying German ships in foreign waters
with fuel, provisions, etc., was built up in peace time but only came
into operation on the outbreak of war. Auxiliary supply bases were
established in the Atlantic Ocean, at New York, Havana, Rio de Janeiro, Buenos Aires, and Las Palmas with smaller centres at St. Thomas,
Para, Bahia, Santos, Pernambuco, Monte Video, Punta Arenas, Teneriffe, Horta and Lome in Togoland. Captain Boy-Ed, the Naval Attaché
at Washington, was in general control of this area. In the Pacific, they
were organised on the West Coast of North and South America, in
China and Japan, and at Batavia, Manila and Tsingtao.

The officer in charge at the main base of each area was responsible
for the quality and quantity of supplies, for the means of transport and
for the requisitioning and equipment of the auxiliary vessels needed
by the warships operating in his area. He had to maintain colliers at
certain rendezvous which were given in the handbook carried by
cruisers so that they knew where to obtain coal without making signals. Besides these rendezvous, others were given where liners could
be fitted out as auxiliary cruisers. One was near the Bahamas and it
was there that the *Kronprinz Wilhelm* met the *Karlsruhe*. Another was
near Trinidada Island and a third, which was never used, somewhere
on the Argentine Coast.

Naval and commercial personnel were also distributed at various
places on the coasts. The latter used their business connections to obtain supply vessels, fuel, stores, etc., and were responsible for chartering
and manning these vessels clearing them from the ports and appoint-
ing super-cargoes. All business transactions undertaken on behalf of
the navy were supervised by them. They enjoyed a great degree of
independence and had to make important decisions on their own

responsibility.

In order that this organisation could begin to function on the outbreak of war, agreements were made with a number of German shipping companies, banks and commercial firms, who undertook to put their steamers, stores and credit at the disposal of German ships in foreign waters as soon as war appeared imminent.

Agreements were also drawn up with shipping companies and business firms regarding the upkeep of stocks of coal or its delivery, in stated quantities, at numbers of places on various coasts. The supply of ammunition to cruisers abroad had also been arranged. As regards the Cruiser Squadron and ships on the Australian and East African Stations, there was a full war-time supply of ammunition in Tsingtao which could be transported elsewhere if necessary. Stocks of charts for auxiliary vessels were kept in a number of commercial centres.

A certain amount of information concerning coaling arrangements has already been given in Chapters 2 and 3, and the following additional remarks are confined to the Cruiser Squadron, the *Emden*, *Koenigsberg*, *Karlsruhe*, *Kaiser Wilhelm der Grosse* and *Kronprinz Wilhelm*. Cruiser Squadron.

Commander Von Knorr, the Naval Attaché at Tokio, was in charge of the auxiliary base in Japan. News of the political situation in Europe at the end of July led him to take immediate measures for meeting the needs of the Cruiser Squadron, in spite of the optimistic views held at the German Embassy. His first step was to interview representatives of business and shipping firms and arrange for the requisitioning of any available steamers and the purchase of coal and stores. On the 31st July, everything was so far arranged that purchases could be concluded on the word being given.

After the outbreak of hostilities, communication with the Cruiser Squadron was difficult owing to the destruction of Yap Wireless Station on 12th August. Commander Von Knorr did not know whether it was still operating in the same area, but it had already been provided with four well-equipped steamers and reliable information on the probable attitude of Japan. He recommended that in view of Japan's probable participation in the war, the Squadron should proceed to West American waters. After Japan declared war he left for San Francisco to take over the auxiliary bases of North West America and there continued to provide for the needs of the Squadron.

The auxiliary supply base at Shanghai was under the orders of Commander Luring of the *Jaguar*. On 1st August, orders were received from the *Emden* to send 5,000 tons of coal to both Pagan and rendezvous A, and also some shipments to rendezvous B; on 6th August, Tsingtao transmitted orders from the Commander-in-Chief that all shipments were to be sent to Pagan, and on 7th August that all were to be sent to rendezvous B.

Lt. Cdr. Von Meeller took command of the auxiliary base at Manila on 6th August, bringing with him the crew of the gunboat *Tsingtao*. It had, however already begun work. On receipt of a telegram from the Cruiser Squadron on 1st August instructing it to begin sending shipments of coal and to advise Batavia and Singapore accordingly, the staff bought up all the coal in Manila belonging to Madrigal & Co., and obtained the first call on supplies expected by that firm. On being informed of these purchases, the commander-in-chief sent the following orders on the night of lst-2nd August:—

Send first 5,000 tons to Pagan, second 5,000 tons to Angaur (collier to cruise up and down to the eastward of Pelew Islands); next 5,000 tons to Zamboanga to await orders from Squadron. Delay further shipments.

On 7th August, the S.S. *Rio Pasig*, sailed under the American flag with 5,000 tons of coal for Pagan. She arrived the day after the Squadron had left, cruised about in search of it for several weeks and was captured off Zamboanga on 15th September by a British destroyer. Her cargo was confiscated by the Prize Court at Hong Kong and she was released.

On the Cruiser Squadron's arrival at Mas-a-Fuera, information regarding German vessels lying in harbours in South-West America and coal supplies were brought by Lt. Riediger in the *Amasis* from Callao. Graf Von Spee had asked for 5,000 tons of coal to be sent to Juan Fernandez, 10,000 tons to Port Low, 10,000 tons a fortnight later to Valparaiso, and 10,000 tons of coal, water and stores to Chilean ports on 20th October. San Francisco was also to report by 25th October whether 20,000 tons of coal and provisions could be sent to South Chile by the end of December. Lt. Riediger was despatched in the S.S. *Yorck* to organise these deliveries. He was informed that the Squadron would be at Juan Fernandez about 27th October and at Port Low on 3rd November, and was to report this to Valparaiso. The general orders given by the *Dresden* regarding equipment and despatch of colliers, etc., were confirmed and supplemented by the commander-in-chief.

Valparaiso supply base sent the commander-in-chief an account of its activities and co-operated with the supply bases at San Francisco and La Plata to meet the Cruiser Squadron's needs. This account showed that, in consequence of the unfriendly attitude of the American authorities in San Francisco, Cdr. Von Knorr had failed to send off the first 15,000 tons of coal to Juan Fernandez and Port Low on the date required, that the *San Sacramento* was bringing the first consignment from San Francisco and that further consignments would follow. The Valparaiso base, also reported that the *S.S. Seydlitz, Santa Isabel, Ramses* and *Memphis* were ready to sail with 12,700 tons of cargo, as already reported by the *Yorck*.

Graf Von Spee's decision to break through to the North Sea was followed by telegraphic instructions from him via Valparaiso to the supply bases at La Plata and New York:—

Send steamers, German if possible, to arrive at port Santa Elena on 5th December with 10,000 tons of coal and provisions for 1,000 men for three months; no oil. Intelligence reports particularly desirable. New York and La Plata are to arrange together for despatch of 20,000 tons of coal, 5,000 to await orders at Pernambuco from 1st January, 15,000 at New York from 20th January; from New York also, provisions for 2,000 men for three months, but only half the oil given in general instructions.

If the Cruiser Squadron had not been destroyed off the Falkland Islands, the 5,000 tons of coal ordered to be in readiness at Pernambuco by 1st January, 1915, might have been delivered there, but its transport from Pernambuco to the Squadron would have proved most difficult, because from October onwards, the British Ambassador had persuaded Brazil not to allow any German steamers to sail if there were the slightest suspicion that they were working for the Cruiser Squadron.

The Argentine Government had also issued an order in October, as a result of British representations, forbidding ships of belligerent countries to embark more coal than could be stowed in the bunkers. In December, they issued a further order that ships of belligerent countries were to declare their destination and their ports of call before leaving Buenos Aires and to give an assurance that they were engaged only in commercial enterprises. Vessels which deviated from the declared route or voluntarily supplied warships with coal were to be treated as auxiliary warships. They, and all vessels belonging to the same company, were henceforth to be refused coal in Argentine ports.

From December, onwards, Uruguay did not allow any vessels to leave Monte Video without a guarantee from the Consulate in question that she was employed on commerce only.

According to the *German Official History*, the alleged "intrigues" of the British Ambassador and Consuls in Chile were overcome at first by the protests of the German Ambassador; but gradually the Chilean Government was subjected to so much pressure, that it became exceedingly difficult for any colliers or provision steamers to sail.

After the *Luxor* and *Memphis* had left Coronel and Punta Arenas without being cleared, the anti-German feeling grew stronger, and at the same time the Allied Governments protested against the prolonged stay of the German Cruisers at Mas-a-Fuera. Von Ercker, the German Ambassador, however, argued that British forces had frequently coaled at bases in Chilean waters, and he prevailed upon Chile not to impose further restrictions. From 1st January, however, Chile allowed war vessels of belligerents to embark only enough coal to take them to the nearest coaling port in another country, and merchant ships were as a rule allowed only to fill their bunkers.

It may be of interest to note that when instructions were issued advising the Cruiser Squadron to return home, the following tentative arrangement? for coaling off Iceland were included in a letter from the Naval Staff dated 10th October:—

> There is a rendezvous line west of Iceland; it begins in 65° 0' N., 26° 0' W., and extends from there 30 miles west (true); a rendezvous has been fixed in 64° 30' N., 26° 0' W. in the event of ice conditions permitting ships to remain on this line. It is said that the west coast of Iceland is free from ice most of the winter and experts report that it is possible to coal from steamers under the lee of the ice barrier. It might be advisable to seek shelter in the bays of Iceland though you would risk being sighted and reported; you might have time to coal before the enemy could come up. The S.S. *Brandeburg* will be sent to the rendezvous line, if she succeeds in getting out of Drontheim, where she is now lying with 5,000 tons of coal; she is fitted with wireless and carries a Merchant Service code book. Endeavours will also be made to despatch colliers of neutral countries to this line, and information regarding them will be communicated by Nauen, Hanover and Nordeich.

When war was declared, the light cruiser *Leipzig* was in Magdalena Bay on the West Coast of Mexico. Before proceeding to join the Cruiser Squadron, she had to make sure of coal supplies, but as German warships seldom visited the North West of America, arrangements for supply in this area had not been thoroughly organised. On 5th August, Captain Haun telegraphed to the San Francisco base, ordering the purchase of 8,000 tons of coal and as much lubricating oil as could be obtained; 5,000 tons of coal and 2,000 kg. of oil were to be despatched at once in the S.S. *Alexandria*, which was due in San Francisco on the 7th August.

A second steamer was to leave eight days later with 3,000 tons of coal and 500 kg. of oil, and eight days later again a third steamer was to be despatched to Saipan (Marianne Islands) with a similar cargo. These instructions were never carried out owing to the lack of suitable ships, lack of coal in San Francisco and lack of money, and the *Leipzig* experienced considerable difficulty in getting sufficient supplies to take her to South American ports.

The light cruiser *Dresden* which was in the West Indies on the outbreak of war obtained all the coal she required from German ships which were summoned from Brazilian ports to meet her at various anchorages on her way south to join the Cruiser Squadron.

EMDEN.

When the *Emden* parted from Admiral Von Spee's Squadron on 14th August, 1914, she was accompanied by the supply ship *Markomannia* carrying 5,400 tons of coal, 45 tons of lubricating oil and provisions. Between that date and her destruction off the Cocos Islands on 9th November, she coaled five times from the *Markomannia* and five times from prizes. Eight of these coalings took place in out of the way harbours such as the Felidu Atoll in the Maldive Islands (*vide* Appendix) or at anchor outside Dutch territorial waters, and two alongside colliers in the open sea.

In the German mobilisation instructions, arrangements had been made for sending supply ships to await orders at neutral ports, but Captain Von Mueller soon realised that this was impracticable in the Dutch East Indies owing, it is stated, to the extremely harsh interpretation of neutrality adopted by the Government of the Netherlands. He soon formed the opinion that they would have to be sent to prearranged rendezvous and that coaling at sea from them or from prizes would be necessary.

Captain Von Mueller suggests that auxiliary vessels accompanying cruisers should, in addition to coal, carry a considerable stock of lubricating oil as this is not easy to obtain from captured ships, about 2 tons of firebricks and the same amount of fireclay, a supply of sheet and angle iron, washing water, livestock, good fenders and securing hawsers. He also states that it may be necessary to coal from the bunkers of captured ships and that appliances enabling the deck of the prize to be cut open should be supplied. When coaling at sea in a slight swell, he found it best to keep the ship head on to the swell by steaming ahead dead slow.

In regard to the question whether the collier should be kept in company, or sent to a pre-arranged rendezvous, Captain Von Mueller remarks:—

> If I had sent my colliers to a rendezvous I should have been free to use the *Emden's* speed to escape from superior forces, without sacrificing the collier as the latter would almost certainly have been captured if kept in company. Nevertheless I considered it better to keep colliers in company for the following reasons:—
>
> 1. A collier alone was liable to capture by an auxiliary cruiser, against which the *Emden* would have afforded effective protection.
>
> 2. If the collier failed to arrive at the rendezvous, the *Emden* might have been placed in a very dangerous position, through lack of coal.
>
> 3. By keeping the collier in company I was able to change my plans unhampered by predetermined rendezvous.
>
> 4. Every favourable opportunity, particularly fine weather could be utilised for coaling.
>
> 5. The collier in company was frequently useful for accommodating the crews of prizes. Whenever two colliers were available I considered it advisable to keep only one in company.

Although Captain Von Mueller's reasons for employing these particular methods are quite clear, it is evident, says the *German History*, that the procedure will largely depend on the particular circumstances of each case, such as the geographical and strategical conditions of the area of operations, the type of collier available and the personality of their masters.

KOENIGSBERG.

The difficulties which the *Koenigsberg* experienced in obtaining supplies of coal limited her activities and were responsible for her return to the Rufiji River on 20th September, 1914, where she was blockaded and finally destroyed. Even before the war commenced, the cable service *via* Zanzibar, which was under British control, became unreliable. For this reason, attempts by the naval commanders to communicate with confidential agents at ports in South Eastern Africa, regarding the despatch of supply ships, were almost entirely unsuccessful. As the agents, themselves did nothing, and as all stocks of coal at ports in South Africa, Portuguese East Africa, and Zanzibar had been commandeered by the British at an early date, only the stocks in German East Africa remained available for supplying the *Koenigsberg* and auxiliary vessels.

Two ships in Dar-es-Salaam, the *Somali* of 2,550 tons and *Konig* of 5,034 tons, were suitable for supply ships, but only the former succeeded in getting to sea and coaling the *Koenigsberg*, once off the Arabian coast and once off Aldabra Island in Madagascar.

KARLSRUHE.

The *Karlsruhe* was in the vicinity of Havana when relations became strained, and her captain issued numerous instructions to the supply base at that port. The North German–Lloyd steamer *Neckar* (9,835 tons) was despatched to the Bahamas on the night of 4th August and the *Spreewald* (3,899 tons) was also sent there from St. Thomas. Both these ships, as well as the *Thor* and *Lorenzo*, were ordered to a rendezvous line to the eastward of Trinidad on 26th August to await the *Karlsruhe*. The German Consul at Tampico was requested to forward 400 tons of fuel oil to the Hamburg-Amerika Line's agent at Havana and the supply base at New York to include supplies of oil in the auxiliary vessels fitted out at that port, 200 tons being the normal amount required for the *Karlsruhe*.

It has already been mentioned (*vide* Chapter 2) that the *Karlsruhe* was separated from her supply ship by the *Suffolk* and *Bristol* and had only just sufficient fuel to reach San Juan de Porto Rico. After coaling at Curacoa, she met the *Patagonia* on the rendezvous line off the Testigos Islands and coaled from her at Maraca Island, Saint Joao and Lavadeira Reef (*vide* Appendix). The supply ships, *Asuncion* with 1,200 tons of coal and the *Crefeld* with 1,000, the former from Santos and the latter from Rio de Janeiro, were met near the Rocas Rock on 31st August. During the two months, she was operating off the northeast coast of Brazil, the *Karlsruhe* had no difficulty in obtaining ample coal from captured ships (*vide* Chapter 2).

KAISER WILHELM DER GROSSE.

The destruction of the *Kaiser Wilhelm der Grosse* was partly due to the delay in sending her colliers (*vide* Chapter 3). The cause of this is worth examining a little more closely in order to draw attention to the very important part which British diplomatic and consular officials may, and in the last war certainly did, play in operations against German raiders. According to the *German History*, the Las Palmas base was seriously handicapped because large ships could not go alongside the moles and the only available lighters were those of the Woermann Line with a total capacity of 1,900 tons.

This difficulty was increased, it is stated, by the British Consul who did his best to hinder loading and unloading. In order to get ships away quickly it became necessary to load them without completely discharging their cargoes. The first ship sent out, the *Walhalla*, embarked 2,000 tons of coal on top of some of her original cargo. Whilst she was loading provisions, the British Consul stirred up discontent by pointing out that if war broke out there would be a shortage of food and a rise in prices.

His efforts apparently bore fruit for when the *Duala* commenced loading, a mob stopped the embarkation of provisions and instead of her full cargo of coal she sailed with only 1,100 tons. By the time, she met the *Kaiser Wilhelm der Grosse* on 15th August this had dwindled to 800. But the raider required 2,000 tons to take her to South America and the delay in getting it led to her destruction.

KRONPRINZ WILHELM.

The *Kronprinz Wilhelm* always coaled in the open sea. This was usually a difficult operation but her captain realised the danger of anchoring off Trinidada Island even before the *Cap Trafalgar* was destroyed there. It often continued for weeks at a time with occasional interruptions. For example, on 12th September, 460 tons were taken from the supply ship *Ebernburg*, and by dint of incessant work 1,018 tons on the 13th and 14th. The 526 tons remaining in that collier were cleared on the 16th and 17th.

Another supply ship, the *Prussia* then came alongside and 685 tons were taken in on the 18th and 19th. Arrangements were made to continue coaling from the *Pontos* on the 21st, but owing to the swell it had to be deferred until the 25th. On that day, 205 tons were taken in, but a great deal of damage was done, including boats' davits broken clean off and against the 205 embarked on that day, 120 had been consumed. Coaling and provisioning continued on these lines for three weeks during which 2,084 tons were embarked from the *Ebernburg*, 685 tons from the *Prussia*, and 1,300 from the *Pontos*. With 98 tons in the bunkers this made a grand total of 4,165 tons. In the meantime, the ship had burnt 2,145 tons, leaving her after all this labour, only half full with 2,020 tons.

At the beginning of the war, coal was easily obtained from South American ports, but as time passed restrictions on German supply ships were tightened up, so that during the first four months, the greater part of her coal and provisions were obtained from prizes. During the second four, she was entirely dependent on that source of supply. It is apparent that the activities of the *Kronprinz Wilhelm* like those of several other raiders, could have been terminated by convoying ships carrying coal.

CHAPTER 5

Intelligence and Communications

The German Intelligence Service which collected and transmitted information to ships in foreign water was closely associated with the supply bases referred to in the preceding chapter. It had been carefully organised in peace time but the Naval Staff realised that difficulties would arise in the event of war with Great Britain owing to her control of cable communications. The oversea wireless system (Nauen, African Colonies and Far Eastern network) is said to have worked well until the stations were put out of action.

Communications between Berlin and the supply bases on the Atlantic and West American Coast were focused on New York which owing to the interruption of the cable service, was largely dependent on the high power American wireless stations at Sayville and Tuckerton.

These two stations were under strict government control and only took cyphered messages if a copy of the code were deposited. They also refused telegrams addressed to belligerent warships.

In spite of the alleged one-sided neutrality of the United States, the energy and experience of Captain Boy-Ed are said to have successfully surmounted these difficulties. In any case, the organisation seems to have maintained communications with the Cruiser Squadron, *Karlsruhe* and *Kronprinz Wilhelm* during the first few months of the war. For example, the *Karlsruhe* received the following message *via* S.S. *Holger* on 2nd of October:—

> From Shanghai. German Cruiser Squadron on the way to Chile. From the Naval Staff. *Dresden* South America West Coast. *Leipzig* Galapagos Islands. *Cap Trafalgar* has been sunk. Rendezvous Line by Rocas Reef, and Trinidada compromised. Punta Arenas reports

S.M.S Cap Trafalgar sunk by H.M.S. Carmarnia

Good Hope, Monmouth, Glasgow sailed 30th September for Chile . . . etc.

The German supply ship *Holger* acted as wireless repeating ship at Pernambuco. This breach of neutrality led to protests from the British authorities and when she slipped out on 1st January, 1915, without clearance papers, steps were taken to prevent merchant ships using wireless in Brazilian harbours.

Las Palmas was another important intelligence centre. After the Emden-Teneriffe cable was cut, plain language telegrams with hidden meanings were sent to Germany *via* the capitals of neutral countries. Communications with the high power wireless station at Kamina in Togoland was severed by the cutting of the Monrovia-Lome cable on 5th August and the Lome-Duala cable on the 9th. From September, onwards, telegrams were usually sent *via* Madrid. Funchal and Horta only accepted ciphered messages during the first few days of the war and plain language messages with hidden meanings did not always reach their destination.

Up to the 7th August, German ships in port were able to transmit signals to ships in the Atlantic but on that date their wireless was sealed by the Spanish authorities. Attempts were then made to communicate with German cruisers by addressing telegrams to imaginary passengers in ships that happened to be within range or to the Austrian Embassy in Madrid, but these were only accepted in cipher up to the 22nd August. Plain language messages with hidden meanings were liable to arouse suspicion and the ship addressed did not always realise they were intended for her. Nevertheless, communication was established by this method with the *Kronprinz Wilhelm*.

Shanghai was the principal intelligence centre in the Far East. Commander Luring, who was in charge of that base, established a news service with Germany which supplied Tsingtao and the Chinese press with reports of events in Europe. He installed a 1.5 kilowatt wireless set in the German ship *Sikiang* which maintained communications with Tsingtao. The Entente Powers protested but it was pointed out that they were using similar stations on shore in Shanghai.

This means of communication proved of great value when the Wusung-Tsingtao and Tsingtao-Chifu cables were cut on the 22nd and 2nd August. After the bombardment of the Yap Wireless Station on 12th August, the surveying ship *Planet* got it working again by the 22nd August but only with a range of 500 miles which was insufficient for communicating with the Cruiser Squadron.

The *Dresden* and *Leipzig* organised an intelligence service off the coast of Chile which depended on the reception and transmission of signals by German ships in Chilian harbours and the use of special call signs and catchwords for communicating with the Cruiser Squadron. Arrangements were also made for certain Peruvian wireless stations to report the movements of British ships. It should be noted that the German intelligence organisation failed to supply Von Spee with any information concerning the approach of Admiral Sturdee's battlecruisers. This was not, however, entirely due to the secrecy of their movements for the German Intelligence Centre at Buenos Aires had already inferred the *Invincible's* arrival at Abrolhos Rock on 24th November, 1914.

This priceless information was to have been sent in writing to Port Saint Elena by one of the German supply ships, but for reasons which are not difficult to guess, no attempt was made to cable it to Punta Arenas or Valparaiso from where it might possibly have been transmitted by wireless. As a matter of fact, Admiral Sturdee did not arrive at Abrolhos until 26th November, two days later. If the date given in the *German History* is correct, it looks as if this intelligence was obtained from a secret Admiralty telegram dated 24th November addressed to Minister, Rio and Intelligence Officer, Monte Video and Pernambuco "for Admiral Sturdee arriving at Abrolhos Rock in *Invincible* on 25th to join squadron." Incidentally the sense of the telegram could have been conveyed without any reference to the *Invincible*, for Admiral Stoddart at Abrolhos Rock had been informed in a telegram of 22nd that the battlecruisers were on their way.

It is important to note that wireless signals made by British cruisers were often of great assistance to the German raiders and the following examples may be quoted to illustrate the necessity for restraint in that method of signalling. When the German Cruiser Squadron first approached the South American Coast, the wireless signals of the *Good Hope, Monmouth* and *Glasgow* were identified from their call signs, and are said to have facilitated bringing them to action at Coronel. Again, when the *Emden* intended coaling at Ulithi Island in the Marianne Group, *en route* to the Indian Ocean, the increasing strength of wireless signals from British cruisers warned her to clear out of that region.

Similarly, when the *Karlsruhe* was awaiting news at the entrance to the Florida Straits on the 3rd August, 1914, the *Berwick's* wireless signals to Nassau indicated that she was approaching and the German raider removed herself to more open waters. The same ship abandoned the rendezvous line off Rocas Reef on 10th September because the wireless signals of a cruiser using the call-sign HG (*Bristol*) appeared to be drawing nearer. Similarly, after capturing the *Farn* with 4,400 tons of coal on 5th October, the *Karlsruhe* altered course to the eastward because wireless signals from the *Bristol* indicated that she was in the vicinity. Incidentally this helped the *Karlsruhe* to capture more ships for it took her on to the route prescribed by the Admiralty to ships bound for Europe. The following remarks appear in the *Karlsruhe's* war diary:—

> Although it is difficult to estimate accurately the distance and movements of enemy vessels from observation of their wireless yet at least some indication of their approximate position can be obtained from their reckless and constant use of wireless. Thus, the enemy systematically helps us to avoid his ships.

The *Kronprinz Wilhelm* also received great assistance from her pursuers' wireless signals, and the fact that she was able to continue her activities for over eight months can be partly traced to this factor. She used to classify all intercepted signals into groups according to whether they emanated from shore stations, enemy warships, enemy merchant ships, neutrals or German auxiliaries.

An attempt was then made to estimate their distance by the strength of their signals and concurrent circumstances. The results were plotted daily on a graph so as to give a general picture of the situation. She mentions that the *Canopus, Dartmouth, Minotaur* and *Highflyer* were very busy signalling to each other for several days round about the 20th December, 1914, in consequence of which the following entry appears in her war diary:—

> The English cruisers are chattering constantly so that one can easily tell whether they are drawing, nearer or not. If they kept quieter or said nothing at all it would be much more disquieting for us.

With the exception of the *Koenigsberg*, which the *German History* criticises for not maintaining silence in the Gulf of Aden, the other German raiders only appear to have used their wireless for communicating with their supply ships on low power at short range and for jamming their victim's calls for help.

It may also be mentioned that the auxiliary cruisers of the 10th

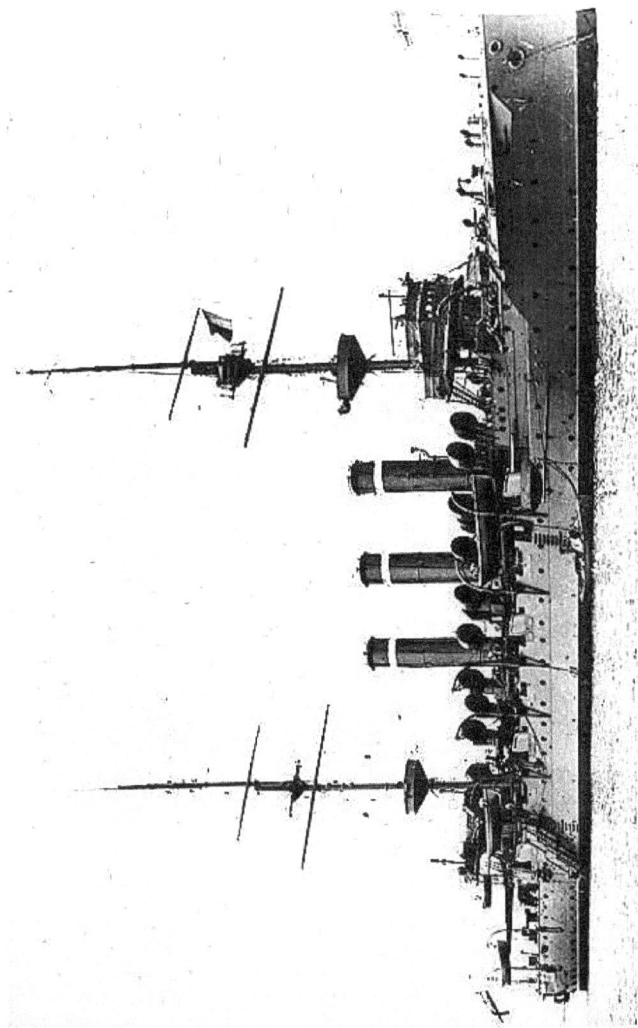

H.M.S. Highflyer

Cruiser Squadron supplied the German directional stations with sufficient data to plot their dispositions and movements and that when possible this information was passed to ships endeavouring to evade the blockade. Also, the *Moewe* intercepted signals from the auxiliary cruisers of the Northern Patrol on both her outward and homeward journeys which provided valuable information concerning their strength and dispositions.

It is true, of course, that we obtained reciprocal benefits from our opponents' wireless signals, but in these particular operations, the balance of advantage lay with the German raiders. It must not be imagined, however, that the captains of British cruisers did not realise the importance of wireless silence in concealing their movements. The true explanation will probably be found in a system of command, developed in the years before the war, which centralised the movements of individual ships in officers commanding squadrons.

Wireless silence was only likely to be attained under a more flexible system which relied on general instructions and the initiative of commanding officers instead of in a succession of detailed orders. In commenting on the destruction of the *Emden* at Cocos Islands, the *German History* lay stress on the necessity of fitting all warships in foreign waters with directional and distance finding apparatus, and modern developments of this kind will enormously increase the importance of wireless silence in operations against raiders.

This precaution also applies to merchant ships for even in the last war, the unnecessary use of wireless sometimes led to their capture. On 5th February, 1916, a plain language message from the *Flamenco* (4,540 tons) reporting her position to Fernando Noronha was responsible for her interception by the *Moewe*. Similarly, the capture of the *Matunga* by the *Wolf* was due to a plain language message giving her time of arrival at Rabaul. Nor were shore stations entirely blameless in this respect for the *Wolf* intercepted a plain language signal from the Naval Transport Officer at Cape Town asking the *Oxfordshire* her time of arrival and number of troops, etc., on board.

There remains one more "Intelligence" question. It was pointed out in Chapters 2 and 3 that misleading reports concerning German raiders sometimes led to the intensive search of areas thousands of miles from their actual position. Similarly, the unfounded rumour that the *Dresden* was in Last Hope Inlet was responsible for much waste of time and energy. It should be realised that the Germans frequently spread false reports of their movements and used bogus wireless signals for the same purpose. When the Cruiser Squadron was off the South American Coast prior to the Battle of Coronel, arrangements were made to give the impression that all its signals emanated from one ship, the *Leipzig*, which had already been reported at Juan Fernandez. Hence the probability is that Admiral Cradock did not suspect the close proximity of Von Spee's Squadron until he actually sighted it, whereas the latter knew the exact composition of the British Squadron from their call signs.

Again, when the Germans left Mas-a-Fuera for the second time, the *Prinz Eitel Friedrich* was left behind with orders to proceed to the southwestward and simulate, during the following fortnight, wireless signals from the Cruiser Squadron. Although this attempt to conceal Von Spee's passage round Cape Horn does not seem to have deceived anyone, the manoeuvre illustrates one of the uses to which wireless may be put. The *Koenigsberg* also transmitted bogus messages to convey the impression that she was at sea accompanied by several steamers so as to conceal her hiding place in the Rufiji River.

Three wireless sets were utilised for this purpose, one of which had been removed from the *City of Winchester*. Using the same call signs on each occasion, she made the usual course, speed, coal, etc., signals. Names of places on the African coast and islands in the Indian Ocean were also inserted in dummy messages which, according to the captain of the *Koenigsberg*, were taken in by British ships and passed to the nearest shore station. The fact that our cruisers wasted a great deal of time in searching out of the way anchorages without any real evidence that they had been used by the *Koenigsberg* seems to confirm his statement.

The *German History* also quotes cases in which ships spread false reports concerning their own movements. For example, when the *Dresden* left the West Indies for South America at the beginning of the war, she sent an incorrect report of her position to San Juan de Porto Rico so as to convey the impression that she was homeward bound. Similarly, when she was lying in Hewett Bay her captain instructed Punta Arenas to spread the report that she had been sighted off Cape de Las Virgines on a northerly course. Again, when the *Karlsruhe* proceeded to Cay Sal Bank just before the outbreak of war, she made arrangements for suitable persons in Havana to spread the report that she would arrive at Tampico on 4th August. Other examples might be quoted but these suffice to show the necessity for caution in examining reports of enemy movements.

Appendix

ANCHORAGES USED BY RAIDERS

PACIFIC OCEAN—NORTH.

Anchorages.	Position.		Remarks.
	Latitude.	Longitude.	
Magdalena Bay	3° 56′ N.	77° 20′ W.	LEIPZIG, 1 Supply Ship.
S. Francisco Bay Light Vessel, California	37° 45′ N.	122° 42′ W.	LEIPZIG.
Ballenas Bay—rock, California ...	26° 42′ N.	113° 39′ W.	LEIPZIG, 1 Supply Ship.
Concepcion Bay—peak, California	26° 45′ N.	111° 46′ W.	LEIPZIG, 1 Supply Ship, coaled from shore.
Guaymas—Isla Parajos	27° 53′ N.	110° 52′ W.	LEIPZIG, 1 Supply Ship.
Yap—Garim Islet	9° 27′ N.	138° 05′ E.	PLANET, CORMORAN.
Ponape—peak	6° 52′ N.	158° 14′ E.	Cruiser Squadron.
Pagan—Apau Bay	18° 08′ N.	145° 46′ E.	Cruiser Squadron and Supply Ships.
Eniwetok atoll—Brown Is., Marshall Is.	11° 21′ N.	162° 21′ E.	Cruiser Squadron and Supply Ships.
Majuro atoll—Marshall Is. ...	7° 06′ N.	171° 21′ E.	CORMORAN, EMDEN, Cruiser Squadron and 4 Supply Ships.
Christmas Is.	1° 59′ N.	157° 28′ W.	Cruiser Squadron and 5 Supply Ships.
Korror Harbour, Angaur, W. Carolines	7° 17′ N.	134° 32′ E.	EMDEN, GEIER, PRINZ EITEL FRIEDRICH, and 2 Supply Ships.
Lamotrek, Carolines	7° 28′ N.	146° 24′ E.	CORMORAN, coaled at quay side.
Malakal Harbour—Channel Pt., Pelew Is.	7° 18′ N.	134° 28′ E.	PRINZ EITEL FRIEDRICH.
Port Langinni—Simaloer Is., Sumatra	2° 39′ W.	96° 11′ E.	EMDEN and 1 Supply Ship.

PACIFIC OCEAN—SOUTH.

Anchorages.	Position.		Remarks.
	Latitude.	Longitude.	
Galapagos Is., Albermarle Is. ...	0° 58′ S.	91° 02′ W. (approx.)	LEIPZIG and 1 Supply Ship.
Galapagos Is., Hood Is.	1° 23′ S.	89° 40′ W.	LEIPZIG.
Galapagos Is., Chatham Is. ...	0° 50′ S.	89° 27′ W.	LEIPZIG and 1 Supply Ship.
Galapagos Is., Wreck Bay ...	0° 54′ S.	89° 36′ W.	LEIPZIG and 1 Supply Ship.
Lobos de Afuera (Lt.)	6° 57′ S.	80° 41′ W.	LEIPZIG and 3 Supply Ships.
St. Nicholas Bay (Puerto San Nicolas)	15° 14′ S.	75° 14′ W.	LEIPZIG and 2 Supply Ships.
Valparaiso	33° 02′ S.	71° 39′ W.	German Cruiser Squadron.
Mas à Tierra (Cumberland Bay) ...	33° 38′ S.	78° 50′ W.	DRESDEN.
Mas à Fuera	33° 46′ S.	80° 46′ W.	DRESDEN, PRINZ EITEL FRIEDRICH, 2 Prizes and 3 Supply Ships.

Anchorages.	Position.		Remarks.
	Latitude.	Longitude.	
Penas Gulf	47° 30′ S.	75° 00′ W. (approx.)	Cruiser Squadron.
St. Qeentin Bay	46° 49′ S.	74° 21′ W.	DRESDEN and 2 Supply Ships.
Kawiung (beacon), New Ireland ...	2° 36′ S.	150° 48′ E.	CORMORAN.
Hermit Is.	1° 30′ S.	145° 04′ E.	CORMORAN.
Mopihaa (Mopelia) Society Is. ...	16° 48′ S.	153° 55′ W.	SEEADLER.
Pageh (Pagi) Is., Sumatra	2° 34′ S.	100° 06′ E. (approx.)	EMDEN and 1 Supply Ship.
Port Refuge—Cocos Is.	12° 05′ S.	96° 52′ E.	EMDEN and 1 Supply Ship.
Alexis Harbour—New Guinea ...	5° 08′ S.	145° 47′ E.	PRINZ EITEL FRIEDRICH and CORMORAN.
Raoul (Sunday Is.)	29° 15′ S.	177° 53′ W.	WOLF and 2 Prizes.
Offak (Fofak) Bay, Moluccas ...	0° 03′ S.	130° 43′ E.	WOLF and 1 Prize.
Nusero Besar (Nusa Bessi) ...	1° 48′ S.	134° 08′ E.	EMDEN and 2 Supply Ships.
Tana Jampea (Jampea) Is. ...	7° 01′ S.	120° 45′ E.	EMDEN and 2 Supply Ships.
Borabora	16° 30′ S.	151° 45′ W.	Cruiser Squadron and 1 Supply Ship.
Nukahiva—Marquesa Is.	8° 56′ S.	140° 00′ W.	Cruiser Squadron and 3 Supply Ships.
Easter Is. (Cook Bay)	27° 08′ S.	109° 25′ W.	PRINZ EITEL FRIEDRICH, 7 Supply Ships and 1 Prize.

ATLANTIC OCEAN—NORTH.

Anchorages.	Position.		Remarks.
	Latitude.	Longitude.	
Cay Sal Bank (Lt.), N. Coast of Cuba	23° 55′ N.	80° 27′ W. (approx.)	KARLSRUHE.
San Juan de Porto Rico	18° 27′ N.	66° 07′ W.	KARLSRUHE.
Santa Anna Bay—Curacao ...	12° 05′ N.	68° 56′ W.	KARLSRUHE.
Maraca Is.—Brazilian Coast ...	2° 05′ N.	50° 20′ W.	MOEWE, 1 Prize, KARLSRUHE and 1 Supply Ship.
Rio de Oro roads, W. Africa ...	23° 40′ N.	15° 55′ W. approx.	KAISER WILHELM DER GROSSE and 4 Supply Ships.

ATLANTIC OCEAN—SOUTH.

Anchorages.	Position.		Remarks.
	Latitude.	Longitude.	
San Joao Is., N. coast Brazil ...	1° 17′ S.	45° 02′ W.	KARLSRUHE and Supply Ships.
Jericoacoara (Jeriquaquara) ...	2° 49′ S.	40° 30′ W.	DRESDEN and 1 Supply Ship.
Rocas Reefs—off coast of Brazil ...	3° 52′ S.	33° 49′ W.	DRESDEN and 2 Supply Ships, KR. PRINZ WILHELM and 1 Supply Ship.
Lavadeira Reef—off coast of Brazil	5° 02′ S.	36° 01′ W.	KARLSRUHE (5 times).
Trinidada Is.—off coast of Brazil	20° 30′ S.	29° 20′ W.	DRESDEN and 5 Supply Ships, CAP TRAFALGAR, EBER, MOEWE, GEIER.
Tova Is., Gulf San Jorge—Argentine	45° 05′ S.	66° 02′ W.	DRESDEN called with 2 Supply Ships.
Cayetano Bay (Gill Bay), Argentine	45° 01′ S.	65° 51′ W.	DRESDEN called with 2 Supply Ships.
Port Santa Elena, Argentine ...	44° 32′ S.	65° 22′ W.	DRESDEN.

TIERRA DEL FUEGO AND MAGELLAN STRAITS AREA.

Anchorages.	Position.		Remarks.
	Latitude.	Longitude.	
Orange Bay (pyramid)	55° 31′ 24″ S.	68° 05′ 24″ W.	DRESDEN and 2 Supply Ships.
Puntas Arenas (beacon)	53° 08′ S.	70° 51′ W.	DRESDEN.
Snug Bay	53° 52′ S.	71° 26′ W.	DRESDEN and 1 Supply Ship.
Sholl Bay	54° 15′ S.	71° 01′ W. (approx.)	DRESDEN and 1 Supply Ship.
Hewett Bay	54° 15′ 40″ S.	72° 21′ 30″ W. (approx.)	DRESDEN and 1 Supply Ship.
Christmas Bay, Stokes Bay ⎫	53° 59′ S.	72° 41′ W. approx.	DRESDEN and 1 Supply Ship.
Sylvester Bay, Stokes Bay... ⎬	S. Coast of Santa Ines Is.		DRESDEN and 1 Supply Ship.
Fox Bay ... ... ⎭	53° 53′ S.	70° 27′ 30″ W. (approx.)	DRESDEN and 1 Supply Ship.
Puerto San Antonio	53° 53′ 36″ S.	70° 54′ 05″ W. (approx.)	DRESDEN and 1 Supply Ship.
San Jose Bay	52° 21′ 20″ S.	74° 27′ 30″ W. (approx.)	DRESDEN and 1 Supply Ship.

INDIAN OCEAN.

Anchorages.	Position.		Remarks.
	Latitude.	Longitude.	
Felidu Atoll, Maldives	3° 30′ N.	73° 31′ E. (approx.)	EMDEN and 2 Supply Ships.
Teladum Mate Atoll, Maldives ...	6° 40′ N.	73° 00′ E.	EMDEN and 1 Supply Ship.
*Addu Atoll, Maldives	0° 35′ S.	73° 05′ E.	EMDEN.
Suvadiva Atoll, Maldives	0° 18′ N.	73° 22′ E.	WOLF and 1 Prize.
Nancoury (Channel), Nicobar Is. ...	7° 26′ N.	93° 42′ E.	EMDEN and 1 Prize.
*Balasor Roads	21° 28′ N.	87° 03′ E.	EMDEN.
Diego Garcia...	7° 21′ S.	72° 27′ E.	EMDEN and 1 Prize.
Bendar Burum Bay, Gulf of Aden...	14° 30′ N.	49° 00′ E.	KOENIGSBERG and 2 Supply Ships.
Hallanya Is., S.E. Arabia	17° 33′ N.	56° 04′ E.	KOENIGSBERG, 1 Supply Ship and 1 Prize.
Soda Is., Khorya Morya Bay ...	17° 28′ N.	55° 54′ E.	KOENIGSBERG and 1 Supply Ship.

86

Plates

PACIFIC OCEAN—SOUTH.

Anchorages.	Position.		Remarks.
	Latitude.	Longitude.	
Galapagos Is., Albermarle Is. ...	0° 58' S.	91° 02' W. (approx.)	LEIPZIG and 1 Supply Ship.
Galapagos Is., Hood Is.	1° 23' S.	89° 40' W.	LEIPZIG.
Galapagos Is., Chatham Is. ...	0° 50' S.	89° 27' W.	LEIPZIG and 1 Supply Ship.
Galapagos Is., Wreck Bay ...	0° 54' S.	89° 36' W.	LEIPZIG and 1 Supply Ship.
Lobos de Afuera (Lt.)	6° 57' S.	80° 41' W.	LEIPZIG and 3 Supply Ships.
St. Nicholas Bay (Puerto San Nicolas)	15° 14' S.	75° 14' W.	LEIPZIG and 2 Supply Ships.
Valparaiso	33° 02' S.	71° 39' W.	German Cruiser Squadron.
Mas à Tierra (Cumberland Bay) ...	33° 38' S.	78° 50' W.	DRESDEN.
Mas à Fuera	33° 46' S.	80° 46' W.	DRESDEN, PRINZ EITEL FRIEDRICH, 2 Prizes and 3 Supply Ships.
Penas Gulf	47° 30' S.	75° 00' W. (approx.)	Cruiser Squadron.
St. Qeentin Bay	46° 49' S.	74° 21' W.	DRESDEN and 2 Supply Ships.
Kawiung (beacon), New Ireland ...	2° 36' S.	150° 48' E.	CORMORAN.
Hermit Is.	1° 30' S.	145° 04' E.	CORMORAN.
Mopihaa (Mopelia) Society Is. ...	16° 48' S.	153° 55' W.	SEEADLER.
Pageh (Pagi) Is., Sumatra	2° 34' S.	100° 06' E. (approx.)	EMDEN and 1 Supply Ship.

90° 95° 100° 105° 110°

CALCUTTA
CHITTAGONG
Ganges R.
BURMA
RANGOON
MOULMEIN
18.IX.
Gulf of Martaban
OF
BENGAL
Aden.
20
19
18
17
16
ANDAMEN IS
MERGUI ARCHIP.
NICOBAR IS.
Coaled 26.X. (Nankauri Harbour)
Kachal
Gt. NICOBAR
23.X.
Southern Ocean
30X
30X
24
6
SIMALOER
Coaled 4-5.IX
31.X.
31.X.
Pini.
Siberut
Coaled 2.XI
N. Pageh I.
S. Pageh I.
1.XI
2.
3.XI
Engano
1.IX.
"Emden."
6.XI.
Cocos
Is.
7.XI
8.XI
9.XI Anchored in Port Refuge (S.Keeling).
Action with Australian cruiser H.M.S. "Sydney".

SIAM
BANGKOK
GULF OF SIAM.
TONKIN
GULF OF TONKIN
HAINAN
CANTON
PARACEL
S. CHINA
FRENCH INDO-CHINA
SAIGON.
"Mousquet" ½ Glenturret
Russ: Cr: Schemtschug.} 28.X.
PENANG I.
STRAIT SETTLEMENTS
MALACCA STR.
27
28
SINGAPORE.
Anambas G. Is
Natoena I.
S. Natoena Is.
BORNEO
SUMATRA
Banca.
Biliton.
Banka Str.
JAVA SEA.
Sunda Str.
Batavia
JAVA
Soerabaya
Samarang
30.VIII
Christmas I.
"Emden."

as aux cruisers.
12.10. Captured by H.M.s YARMOUTH
sunk
sunk
14.9. sent to Calcutta
13.9. sunk
sunk
released
"
sunk
"
released
sunk
released
sunk
sent to Colombo 27.9.
9.11. sunk
sunk
"
released.
sunk
"
released
19.10. sunk.
19.10. released
11.12. captured by H.M.S Himalaya
sunk
"
released.
sunk.
sent to Sibang.

100°

PLATE. I. O.U.633Y(40)

TRACK OF GERMAN CRUISERS

S.M.S "EMDEN"

AND

S.M.S. "KÖNIGSBERG".

1914.

115° 120° 125° 130° 135°

25°

HONG-KONG

EL I⁵

20°

LUZON

SEA

PACIFIC OCEAN. 15°

PHILIPPINE I⁵

MINDORO SAMAR

PANAY

PALAWAN NEGROS 10°

Balabac Str. MINDANAO. Palau I⁵

Sulu 13.VIII. 18
Archip:

5°

CELEBES SEA. 21 20.VIII

22 "Emden"

Morotai.

Halmahera.

0°

Soela I⁵ 23

CELEBES Ceram

Buru NEW GUINEA.

BANDA SEA

24.VIII

FLORES SEA.

"Emden" 26 Wetar

28 27 "Emden" ARAFURA SEA.

Lombok FLORES Alor 25. 10°

Lombok Str. SOEMBAWA TIMOR

SOEMBA SAWOE TIMOR SEA. MELVILLE I⁵

DARWIN.

15°

AUSTRALIA. 20°

120° 138°

REVIEW OF GERMAN RAIDING OPERATIONS

PREPARED BY NAVAL STAFF (H/S). 1939.

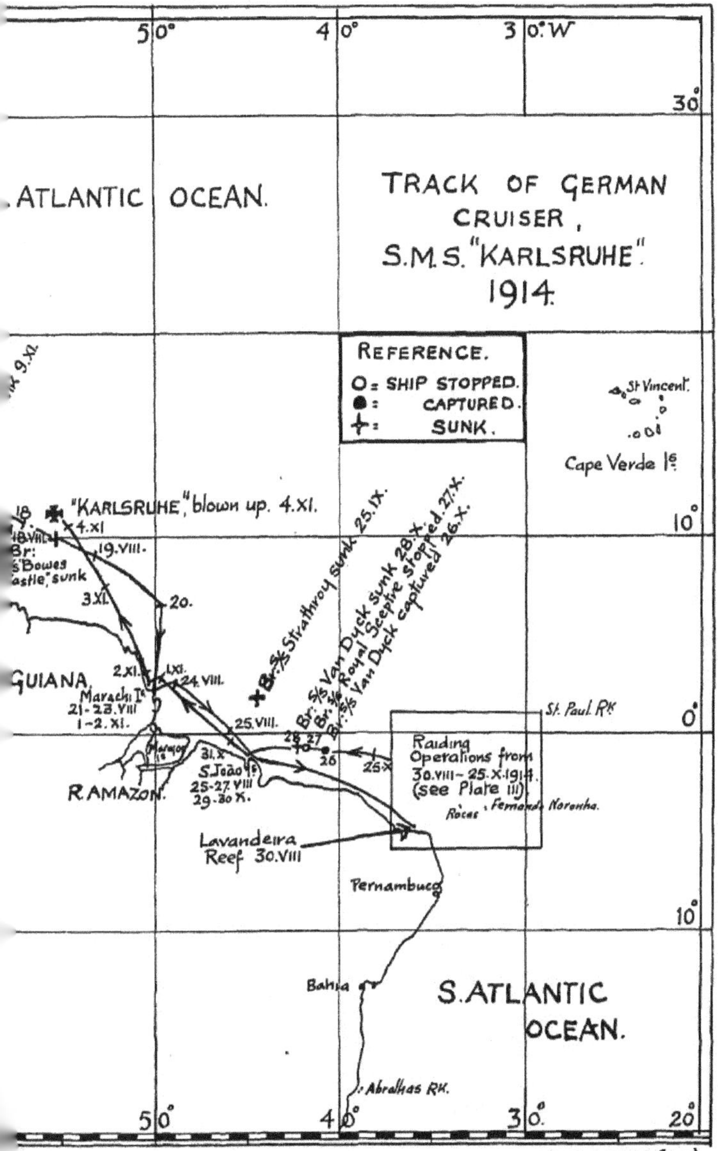

50°   40°   30° W

30°

ATLANTIC | OCEAN.

TRACK OF GERMAN CRUISER, S.M.S. "KARLSRUHE". 1914.

REFERENCE.

O = SHIP STOPPED.
● = CAPTURED.
✝ = SUNK.

St. Vincent.

Cape Verde Is.

"KARLSRUHE", blown up. 4.XI.

10°

18
18.VIII.
Br:
s'Bowes
astle" sunk

✝ 4.XI

19.VIII.

3.XI.

20.

SS Strathroy sunk. 25.IX.

Br: Van Dyck sunk 28.X.X.
Br: Royal Sceptre stopped. 26.X.
S.S. Van Dyck captured 27.X.

GUIANA,

2.XI.
Maracha I.
21-23.VIII
1-2.XI.

1.XI.
24.VIII.

25.VIII.

St. Paul R.K.

0°

31.X.
S.João Is.
25-27.VIII
29.30.X.

25.27
26

25.X

Raiding Operations from 30.VIII - 25.X.1914. (see Plate III.)

R. AMAZON.

Roças

Fernando Noronha.

Lavandeira Reef 30.VIII

Pernambuco

10°

Bahia

S. ATLANTIC OCEAN.

Abralhas R.K.

50°   40°   30°   20°

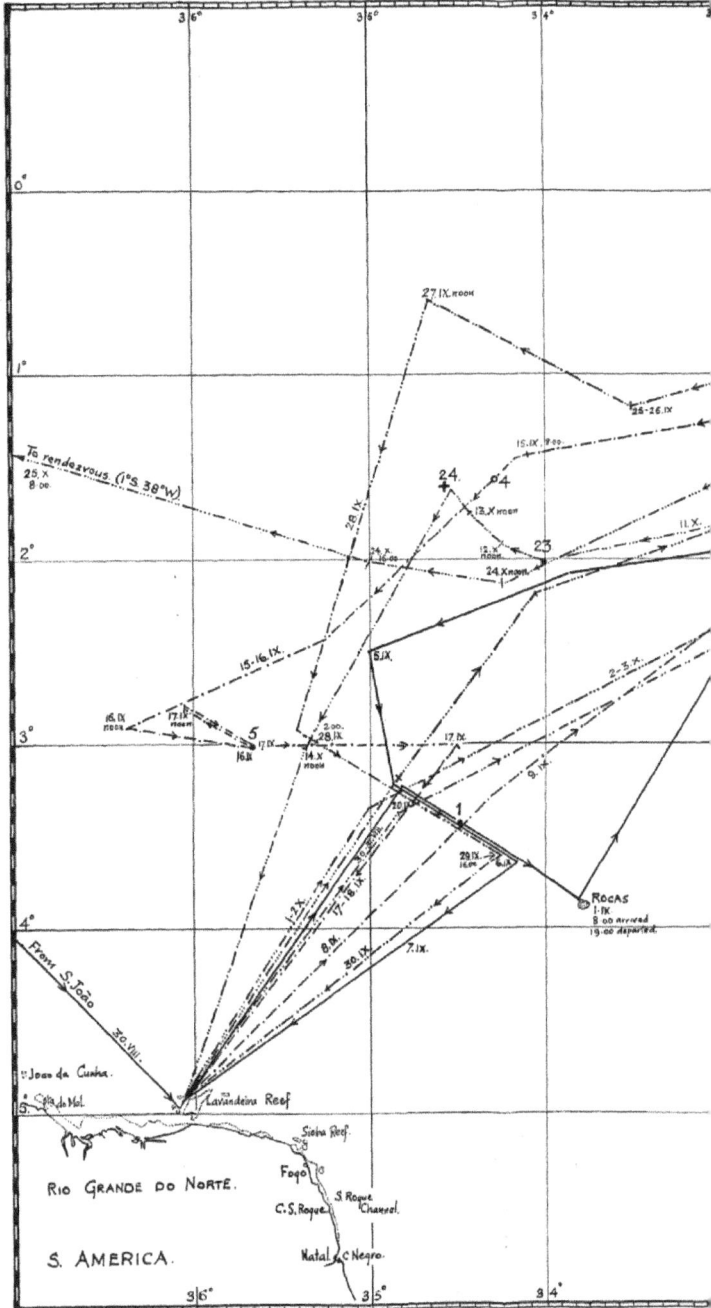

0°

1°

27.IX. noon

25-26.IX

15.IX. 9·00

To rendezvous (1°S. 38°W)
25.X
8·00

24
4

13.X noon

28.IX

11.X.

2°

24.X
16·00

12.X
noon

23

24.X noon

15-16.IX.

5.IX.

16.IX
noon

17.IX
noon

5

2·00.
28.IX.

17.IX

9.IX.

2-3.X.

3°

16.IX

14.X.
noon

20.IX

1

28.IX.
16·00

Rocas
1·IX
8·00 arrived
19·00 departed.

From S.João

30.VIII.

8.IX.

26.IX.

7.IX.

4°

Joao da Cunha.

Pta do Mel.

Lavandeira Reef

Sioba Reef.

5°

Fogo

RIO GRANDE DO NORTE.

C.S.Roque.

S.Roque
Channel.

Matal

C.Negro.

S. AMERICA.

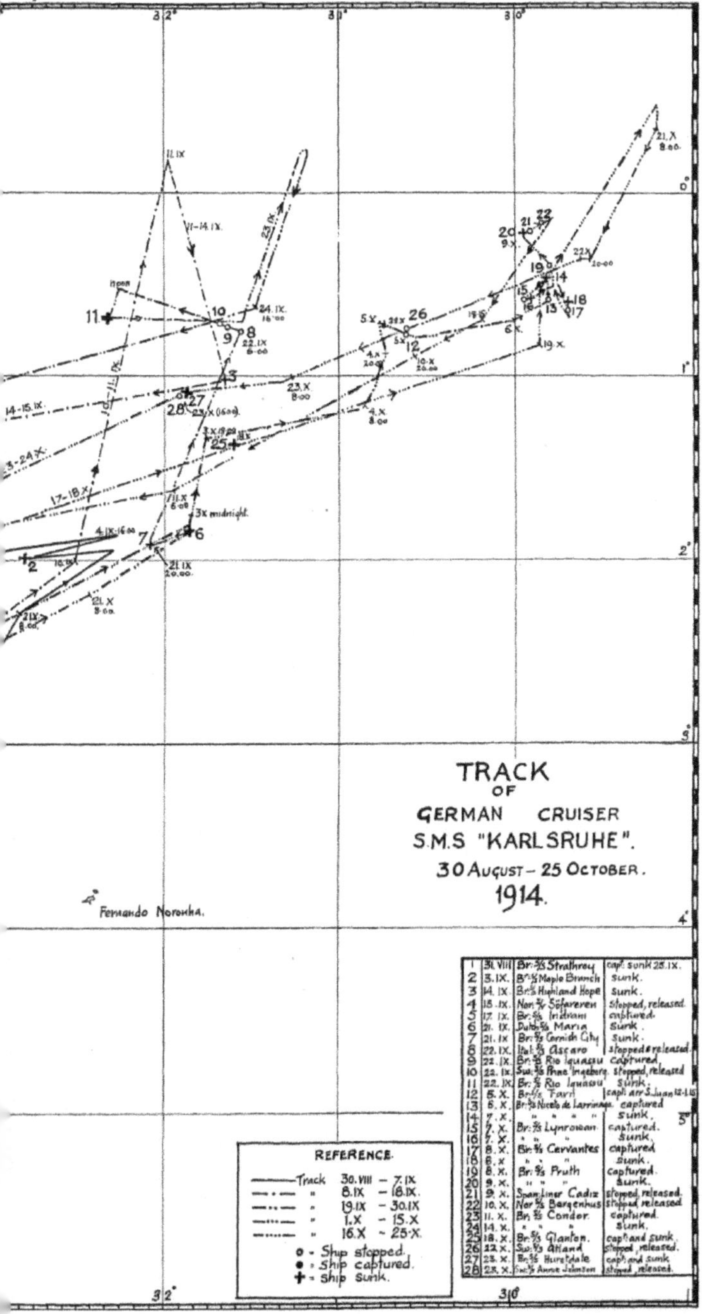

32°
31°
30°
0°
1°
2°
3°
4°
5°
TRACK
OF
GERMAN CRUISER
S.M.S "KARLSRUHE".
30 AUGUST – 25 OCTOBER.
1914.
Fernando Noronha.
REFERENCE.
Track 30.VIII – 7.IX
" 8.IX – 18.IX.
" 19.IX – 30.IX
" 1.X – 15.X
" 16.X – 25.X.
o - Ship stopped.
• - Ship captured.
✝ - Ship sunk.

1	31. VIII	Br. S/S Strathroy	capt. sunk 25.IX.
2	3. IX.	Br. S/S Maple Branch	sunk.
3	14. IX.	Br. S/S Highland Hope	sunk.
4	15. IX.	Nor. S/V Söfareren	stopped, released.
5	17. IX.	Br. S/S Indrani	captured.
6	21. IX.	Dutch S/S Maria	sunk.
7	21. IX	Br. S/S Cornish City	sunk.
8	22. IX.	Ital. S/S Ascaro	stopped & released.
9	22. IX.	Br. S/S Rio Iguassu	captured.
10	22. IX.	Sw. S/S Prinz Ingeborg.	stopped, released
11	22. IX.	Br. S/S Rio Iguassu	sunk.
12	5. X.	Br. S/S Farn	capt. arr S. Juan 12.1.15
13	6. X.	Br. S/S Niceto de Larrinaga.	captured
14	7. X.	" " " "	sunk.
15	7. X.	Br. S/S Lynrowan.	captured.
16	7. X.	" " "	sunk.
17	8. X.	Br. S/S Cervantes	captured
18	8. X	" " "	sunk.
19	8. X.	Br. S/S Pruth	captured.
20	9. X.	" " "	sunk.
21	9. X.	Span. Liner Cadiz	stopped, released.
22	10. X.	Nor S/S Bargenhus	stopped, released
23	11. X.	Br. S/S Condor.	captured.
24	14. X.	" " "	sunk.
25	18. X.	Br. S/S Glanton.	capt. and sunk.
26	22. X.	Sw. S/S Atland	stopped, released.
27	23. X.	Br. S/S Hurstdale	capt. and sunk.
28	23. X.	Sw. S/S Annie Johnson	stopped, released.

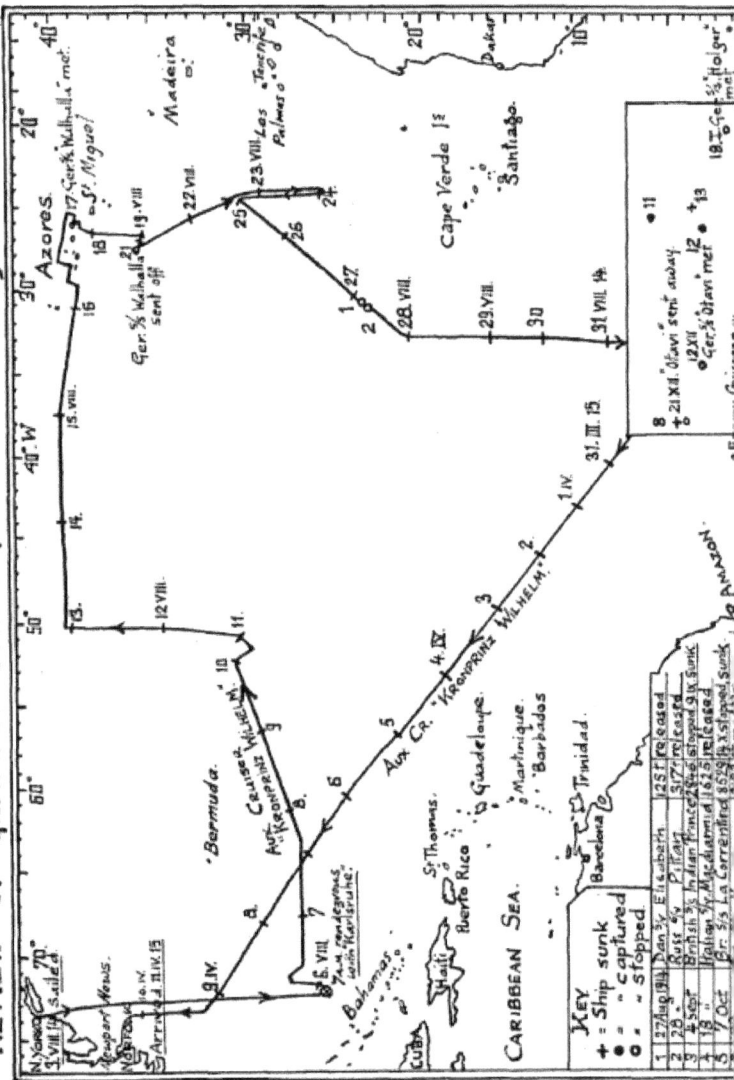

REVIEW OF GERMAN RAIDING OPERATIONS. 1914–18. O.U.633Y(40)

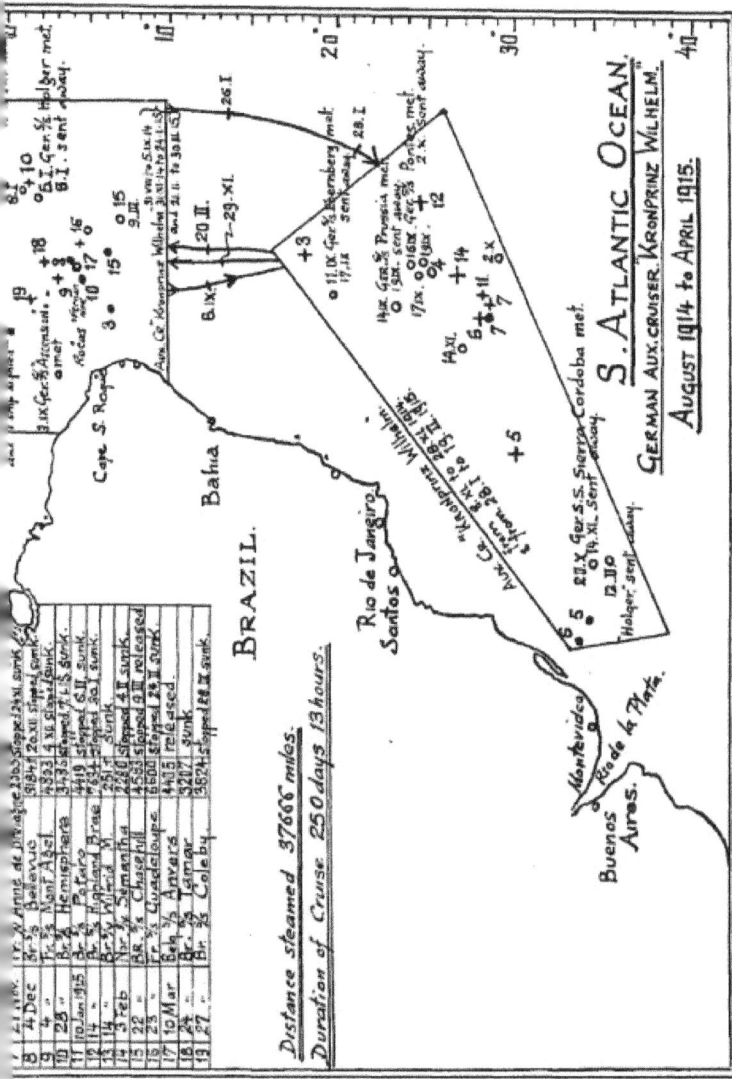

S. ATLANTIC OCEAN.

GERMAN AUX. CRUISER "KRONPRINZ WILHELM."

AUGUST 1914 to APRIL 1915.

PLATE. IV.

BRAZIL.

Cape S. Roque

Bahia.

Rio de Janeiro

Santos

Montevideo

Rio de la Plata.

Buenos Aires.

Distance steamed 37666 miles.

Duration of Cruise 250 days 13 hours.

REVIEW OF GERMAN RAIDING OPERATIONS. 1914-18.

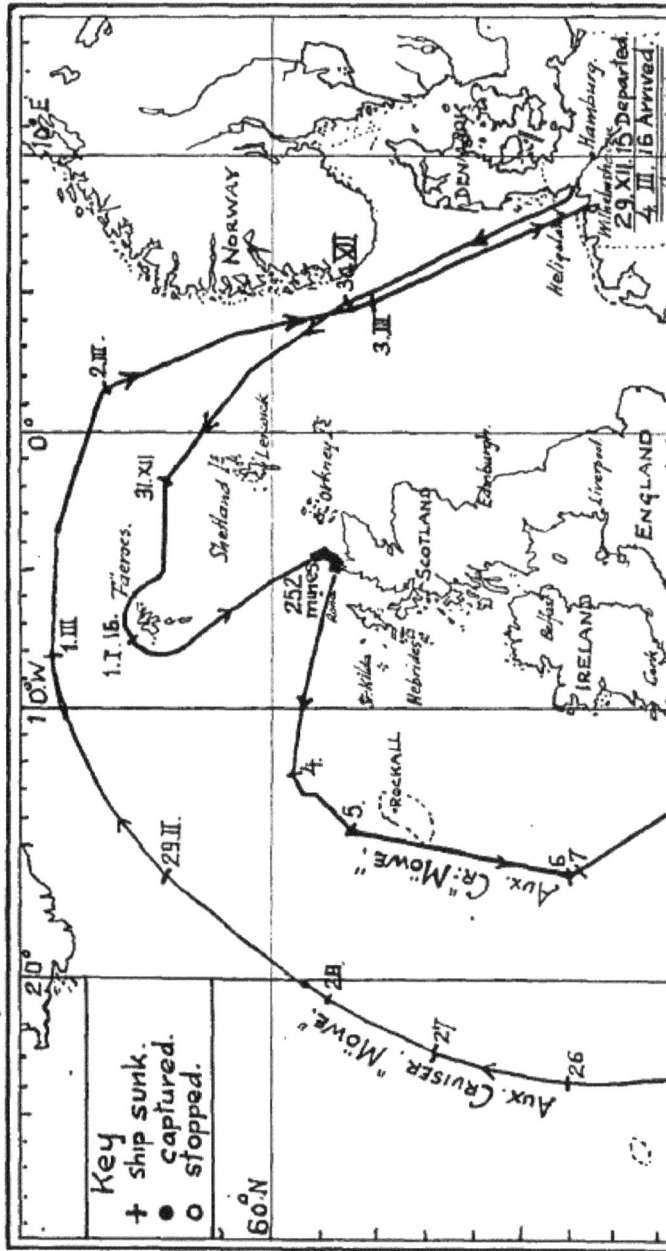

PLATE VI.

Key
+ ship sunk.
● captured.
○ stopped.

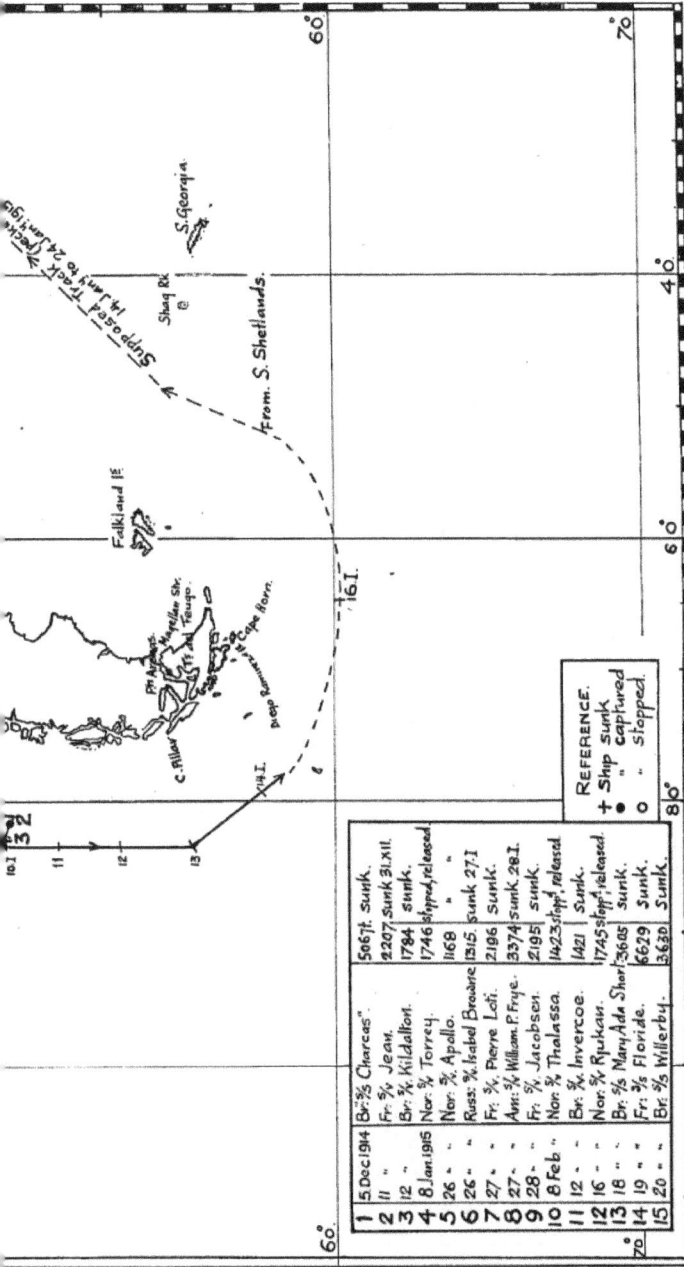

60°   70°   40°   60°   80°

S. Georgia.

Shag Rk.

from S. Shetlands.

Supposed Track 14 Jan. to 24 Jan. 1915

Falkland Is.

Pt Ambrose.   Magellan Str.   Tierra.

C. Pillar.   Cape Horn.   Diego Ramirez.

16.I   14.I   161

10   11   12   13   32

REFERENCE.

+	Ship sunk
●	" captured
○	" stopped

No.	Date		Tonnage	Fate
1	5.Dec.1914	Br. S/S "Charcas".	5067t.	sunk.
2	11 "	Fr. S/v Jean.	2207	sunk 31.XII.
3	12 "	Br. S/v Kildalton.	1784	sunk.
4	8.Jan.1915	Nor. S/v Torrey.	1746	stopped, released
5	26 "	Nor. S/v Apollo.	1168	"
6	26 "	Russ: S/v Isabel Browne	1315	sunk 27.I
7	27 "	Fr. S/v Pierre Loti.	2196	sunk.
8	27 "	Am: S/v William P.Frye.	3374	sunk. 28.I
9	28 "	Fr. S/v Jacobsen.	2195	sunk.
10	8.Feb "	Nor. S/v Thalassa.	1423	stopped, released
11	12 "	Br. S/v Invercoe.	1421	sunk.
12	16 "	Nor. S/v Rjukan.	1745	stopped, released.
13	18 "	Br. S/S Mary Ada Short	3605	sunk.
14	19 "	Fr. S/S Floride.	6629	sunk.
15	20 "	Br. S/S Willerby.	3630	sunk.

O.U.6339/(40)

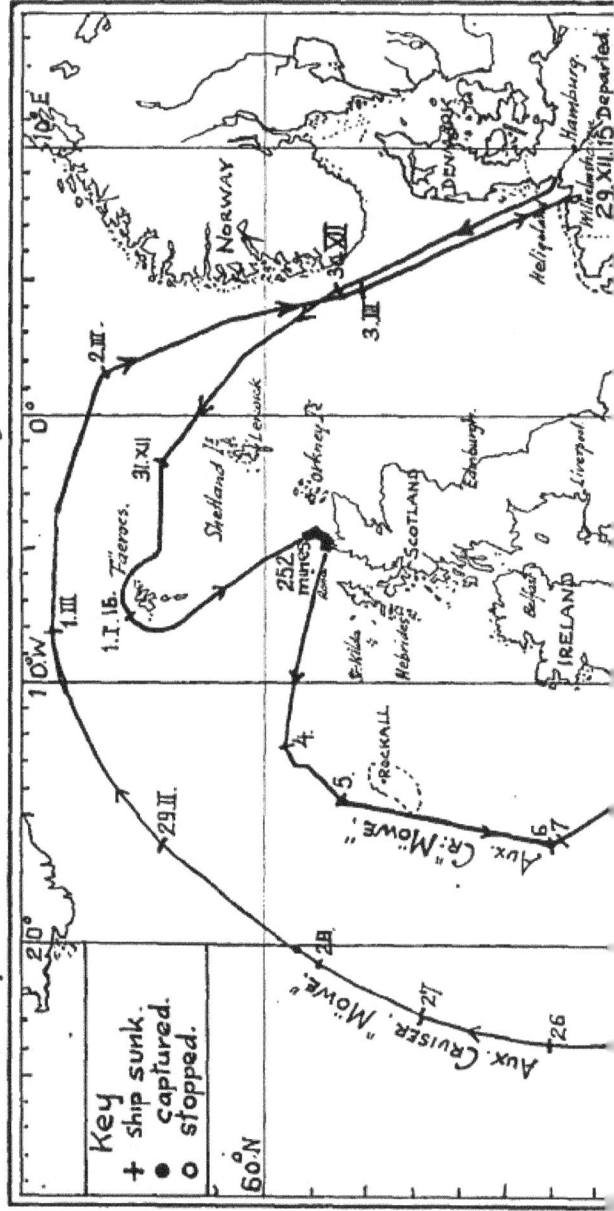

REVIEW OF GERMAN RAIDING OPERATIONS. 1914-18.　PLATE VI.

TRACK OF AUX: CRUISER
"MÖEWE"
NORTHERN PORTION.

FIRST VOYAGE.
29 Dec 1915 – Jan 14. 1916

Outward route ————
Homeward route ↠↠↠
21. Feb? 1916 to 4th Mar. 1916

4. III. 16 Arrived.
GERMANY.

HOLLAND

ENGLAND
London
Pembroke
C. Clear
Corke
Pembroke
St. Ives
S. Wight
Plymouth
Portsmouth

8.I.
9.I.

ITALY.
Gulf of Lyons.
CORSICA
SARDINIA
SICILY
Tunis 10°

238 mines
10
Bay of Biscay.

SPAIN
C. Finisterre.
Vigo
Oporto
PORTUGAL.
C. St Vincent.
1° W.
0

Balearic Is.

7.I. 11.I.
1.
2.

1. "Farringford"
2. Corbridge
3. Dromonby
4. Author
5. "Trader."

2
4
13.I
5   3
1° W.

See Southern track

25.II.
15 ✝ SAXON PRINCE.
24.II ✝ MARONI.
23
22
21.II
S. Miguel
Sta Maria
Azores
Terceira

50°
40°

PREPARED BY NAVAL STAFF (H/S) 1939.

(F.9734) FISH & CROSS LTD

O.U. 6334 (40)

MOEWE'S RAIDS 29.XII.15 to 4.III.1916.

#	Date			Flag	Ship	Tonnage	Fate
1	11 Jan 1916			British	⁹/s Farringford	3146 t	sunk.
2	11	"	"	Br:	s/s Corbridge	3687 t	capt. 30.I sunk
3	13	"	"	Br:	⁹/s Dromonby	3627 t	sunk
4	13	"	"	Br:	s/s Author	3496 t	sunk.
5	13	"	"	Br:	s/s Trader	3608 t	sunk
6	15	"	"	Br:	⁹/s Ariadne	3035 t	sunk
7	15	"	"	Br:	⁹/s Appam	7781 t	capt. 17.I released.
8	16	"	"	Br:	⁹/s Clan Mactavish	5816 t	sunk after action.
9	22	"	"	Br:	s/ Edinburgh.	1473 t	Sunk.
10	4 Feb.	"		Belg:	s/s Luxembourg	4322 t	sunk.
11	6	"	"	Br:	⁹/s Flamenco	4540 t	sunk.
12	8	"	"	Br:	⁹/s Westburn.	3300 t	captured 23.II at St. Cruz,.
13	9	"	"	Br:	⁹/s Horace.	3335 t	sunk.
14	24	"	"	Fr:	s/ Maroni.	3109 t	sunk.
15	25	"	"	Br:	s/s Saxon Prince	3471 t	Sunk.

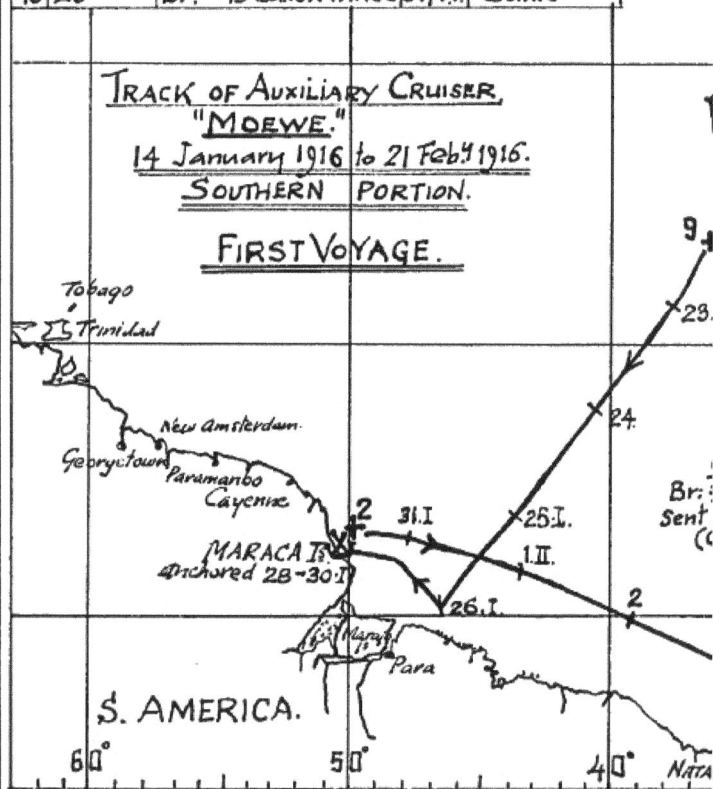

TRACK OF AUXILIARY CRUISER
"MOEWE."
14 January 1916 to 21 Feb.y 1916.
SOUTHERN PORTION.

FIRST VOYAGE.

Tobago

Trinidad

New Amsterdam.

Georgetown

Paramanbo

Cayenne

2   31.I

24.

25.I.

MARACA B.
Anchored 28-30.I

1.II.

9.

23.

Br:
Sent
Co

26.I.

2

Marap

Para

S. AMERICA.

60°   50°   40°   NATA

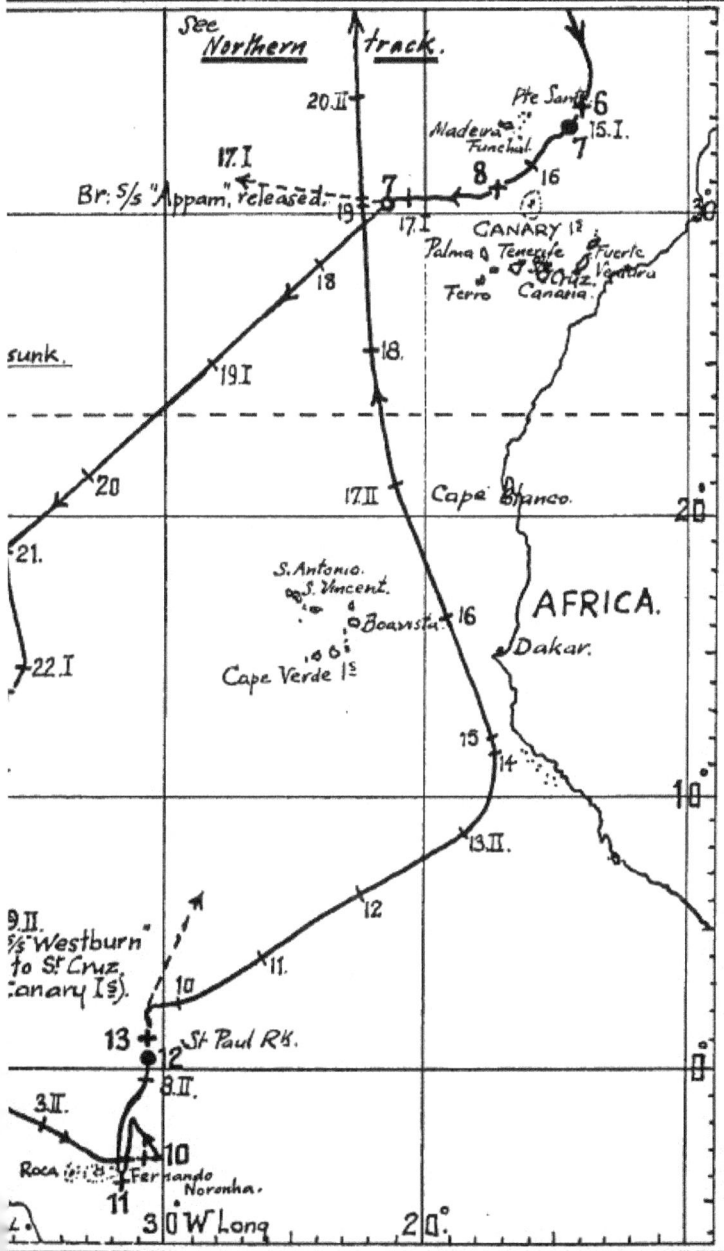

See
Northern   track.

20.II

Pte Santo 6
15.I.
Madeira 7
Funchal.
8   16

17.I
Br. S/s "Appam", released.
19   7
17.I   CANARY I⁵
Palma Tenerife Fuerte
Cruz Ventura
Ferro Canaria.
18

18.

sunk.

19.I

20

21.

17.II   Cape Blanco.   20°

S. Antonio.
S. Vincent.
Boavista   16
Cape Verde I⁵   AFRICA.
Dakar.

22.I

15
14   10°

13.II.

12

9.II.
S/s "Westburn"
to St Cruz,
Canary I(s).   11.

10

13   St Paul R⁵.
12
8.II.

3.II.

10
Roca   Fernando
Noronha.
11   3 0 W Long   2 0°

O.U. 633Y(40)

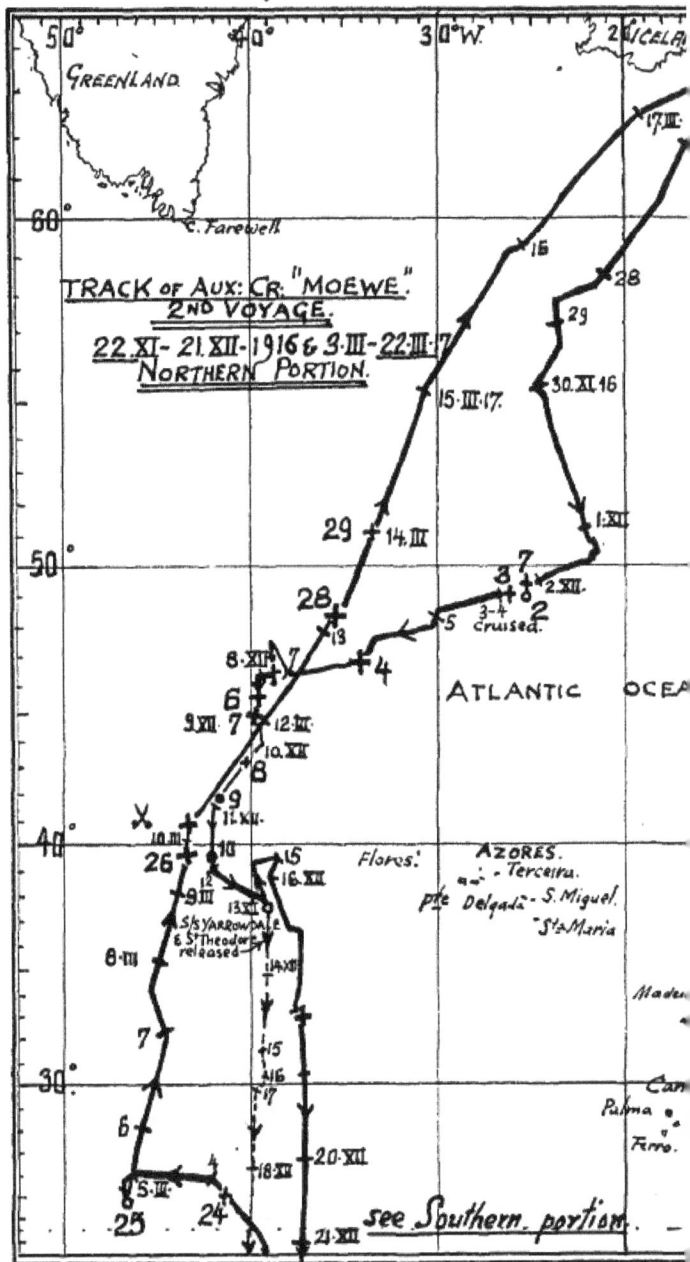

TRACK OF AUX: CR. "MOEWE".
2ND VOYAGE.
22.XI - 21.XII.1916 & 3.III - 22.III.7
NORTHERN PORTION.

ATLANTIC OCEA

AZORES.
Terceira.
Flores.
Ponta Delgada - S. Miguel.
"Sta Maria"

Madei

Can
Palma
Ferro.

see Southern portion.

PREPARED BY NAVAL STAFF (H/S) 1939   (F9734) FOSH & CROSS L.TD

Map labels:

18.III
26.XI Faröes
27.XI
25.XI
19
Shetland Is.
NORWAY
SWEDEN
Orkney Is.
Hebrides
SCOTLAND
NORTH SEA.
Fanö
Heligoland
KIEL
20
23
DENMARK
IRELAND
ENGLAND
HOLLAND
GERMANY.
Scilly, Ushant
Brest
Bay of Biscay
C.ortegal
C Finisterre
SPAIN.
PORTUGAL
FRANCE
CORSICA
ITALY
Balearic Is.
SARDINIA.
C.St Vincent
C.Spartel
Gibraltar
MOROCCO
Fuerte Ventura.
Canaria

Departed 22.XI.16.
Arrived 22.III.17.

Key
+ ship sunk
• captured
○ stopped.

	Date	Flag/Type	Name	Tons	Fate
1	2 Dec 16	Br: s/s	Voltaire	8518	sunk.
2	4 " "	Belg. s/s	Samland	9784	stopped released
3	4 " "	Norw. s/s	Halbjörg	2588	sunk
4	6 " "	Br: s/s	Mount Temple	9792	"
5	8 " "	Br: s/s	Duchess of Cornw:	152	"
6	8 " "	Br: s/s	King George	3852	"
7	9 " "	Br: s/s	Cambrian Range	4235	"
8	10 " "	Br: s/s	Georgic	10077	Capt. 31.XII &
9	11 " "	Br: s/s	Yarrowdale	4652	sunk 14.11.17.
10	12 " "	Br: s/s	Saint Theodore	4992	
11	18 " "	Br: s/s	Dramatist	5415	sunk
12-23	see Southern Portion.				
24	4 Mar 17	Br: s/s	Rhodanthe	3061	sunk
25	5 " "	Nor: Bk	Edderside	1347	stopped, released
26	10 " "	Br: s/s	Esmeraldas	4678	sunk
27	10 " "	Br: s/s	Otaki	9575	
28	13 " "	Br: s/s	Demeterton	6048	sunk.
29	14 " "	Br: s/s	Governor	5524	sunk.

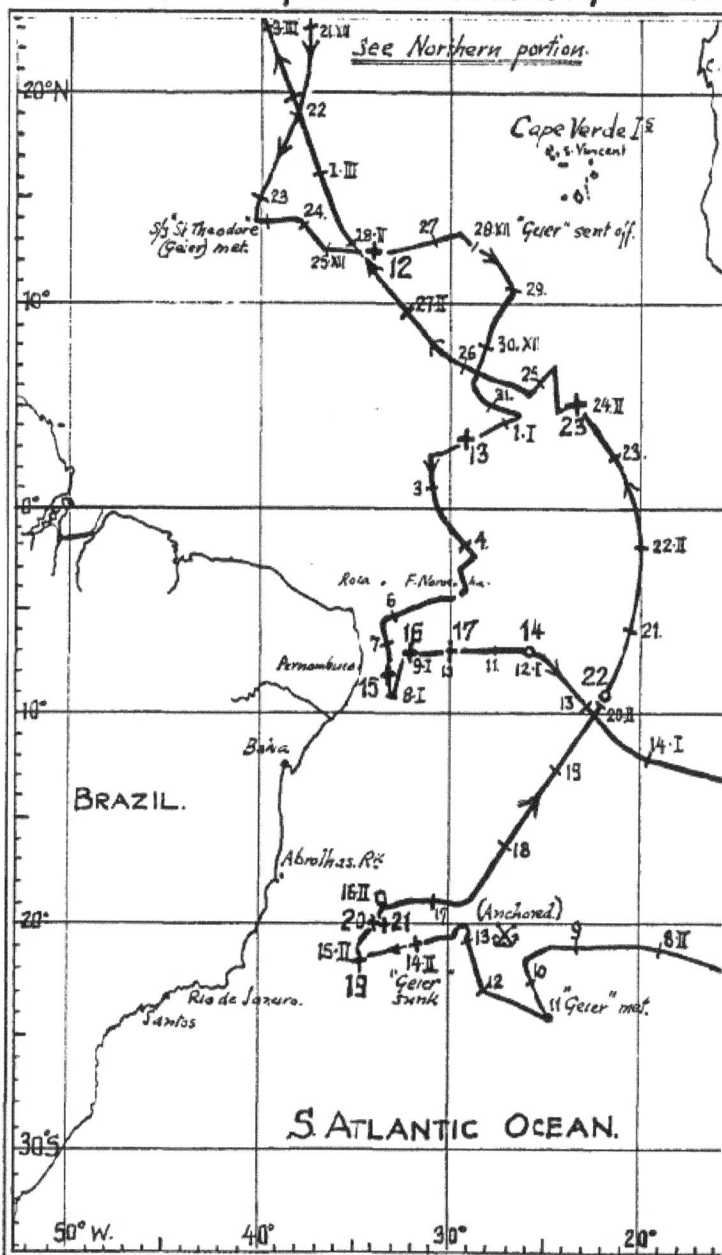

See Northern portion.

20°N

3·III   21·XII

22

Cape Verde Is
S. Vincent

1·III

23   24.   19·IV   27   28·XII "Geier" sent off.

S.S. "St Theodore"
(Geier) met.   25·XI   12   29.

10°   27·II

26   30·XI

25

31.   24·II

1·I   23

13   23.

3   22·II

0°   4.

Roca   F. Naronha.

6   21.

7   16   17   14

15   9·I   11   12·I   22

Pernambuco   8·I   13   20·II

10°   14·I

Bahia.

19

BRAZIL.   18

20°   Abrolhos Rs.

16·II   17   (Anchored.)

20   21   13

15·II   14·II   13   9   8·II
19   "Geier"   12   10
Sunk   11 "Geier" met.
Rio de Janeiro.
Santos

S. ATLANTIC OCEAN.

30°S

50° W.   40°   30°   20°

Blanco

12	26 Dec 16	Fr. Bk: "Nantes"	2679 H	sunk
13	2 Jan 1917	" " Asnières	3103	"
14	5 " "	Jap. S/s Hudson Maru	3798	121 released
15	7 " "	Br: S/s Radnorshire	4310	81 sunk
16	9 " "	" " Minieh	2890	sunk
17	10 " "	" " Netherby Hall	4461	"
18	24 " "	Nov: S/s Tysla	4676	stopped released
19	15 Feb Y:	Br: S/s Brecknockshire	8423	sunk
20	16 " "	K " French Prince	4766	"
21	16 " "	" " Eddie	2652	"
22	20 " "	Nor: Bk: Dagny	1115	stopped released
23	24 " "	Br: S/s "Katherine"	2926	sunk.

Key
+ Ship sunk.
● captured.
○ stopped.

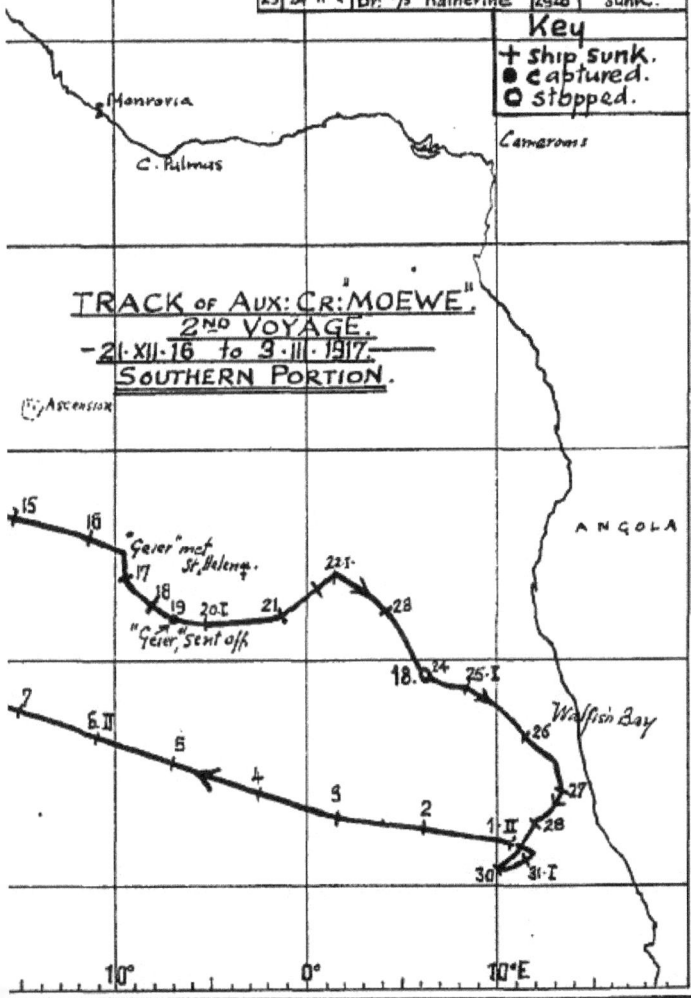

Monrovia
C. Palmas
Cameroons

TRACK of Aux: Cr. "MOEWE"
2ND VOYAGE.
21·XII·16 to 3·II·1917.
SOUTHERN PORTION.

Ascension

15 16
"Geier" met St. Helena.
17
18 19 20·I 21
"Geier" sent off
22·I
28
18·● 24 25·I
ANGOLA
26 Walfish Bay
2 6·II
5 4 3 2 1·II 27 28
30 31·I

10°   0°   10°E

O.U.633Y(40).

REVIEW OF GERMAN RAIDING OPERATIONS. 1914-18.

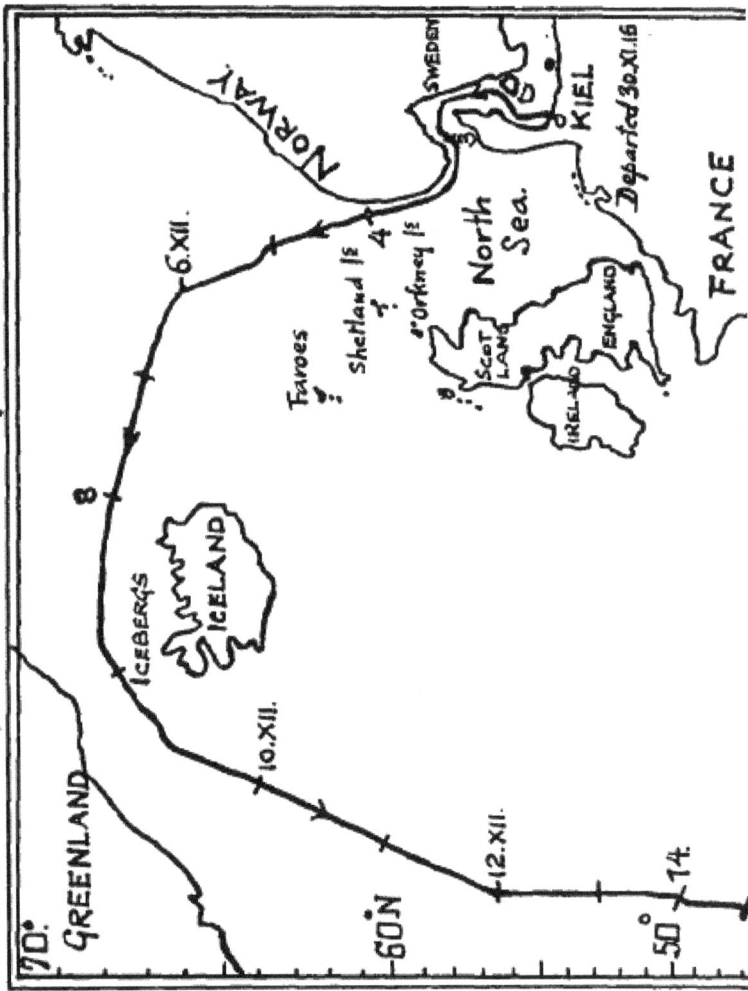

GREENLAND

70°

ICEBERGS

ICELAND

8

6.XII.

Faroes

Shetland Is

Orkney Is

NORWAY

SWEDEN

KIEL

Departed 30.XI.16

North Sea.

ScotLAND

IRELAND

ENGLAND

10.XII.

60°N

12.XII.

50°

14.

FRANCE

ITALY.

SPAIN

AFRICA.

Canary Is

Cape Verde Is

See Southern portion.

Azores.

16.XII.

18.

20.XII.

30

20

40

10 A0

22

24

26.xi

TRACK of AUX: CRUISER "WOLF."
NORTHERN PORTION
30 NOVEMBER to 26 DECEMBER 1916.
Outward Bound.

10°W

0°

10°E.

PLATE. X.
O.U. 633Y(40)

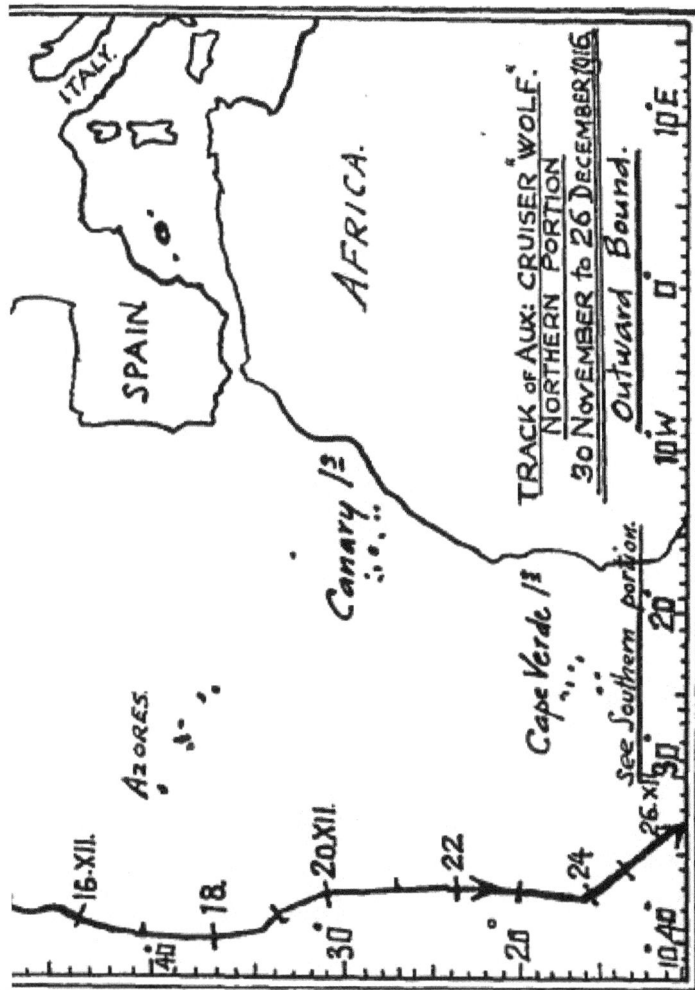

Prepared by Naval Staff. (H/S). 1939.

(F.9734) FOSH & CROSS LTD

REVIEW OF GERMAN RAIDING OPERATIONS . 1914-18.

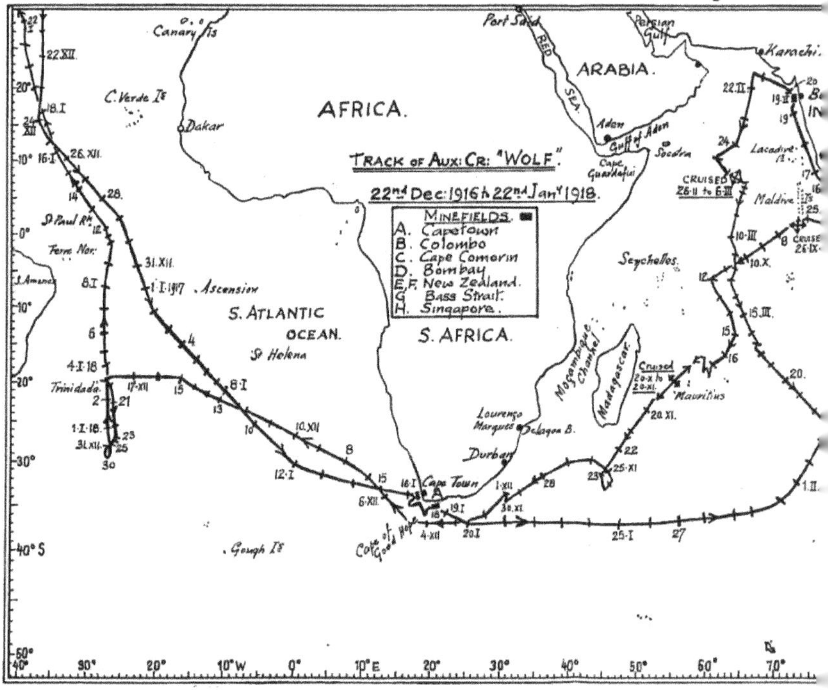

Canary Is.

Port Said

Persian Gulf

Karachi

ARABIA

AFRICA.

C. Verde I⁸

Dakar

RED SEA

Aden

Gulf of Aden

Socotra

Cape Guardafui

Lacadive Is.

Maldive Is.

CRUISED 26·II to 6·III

TRACK OF AUX: CR: "WOLF".
22ⁿᵈ Dec: 1916 & 22ⁿᵈ Janᵞ 1918.

MINEFIELDS.
A. Capetown
B. Colombo
C. Cape Comorin
D. Bombay
E. New Zealand.
F. Bass Strait.
G. Singapore.
H.

S⁴ Paul R⁵

Fern Noc

S. Amaro

Seychelles

S. ATLANTIC
OCEAN.

S⁴ Helena

Ascension

S. AFRICA.

Mozambique Channel

Madagascar

CRUISED 20·X to 20·XI

Mauritius

Trinidada

Lourenço Marques

Delagoa B.

Durban

Gough I⁸

Cape Town

Cole of Good Hope

CRUISE 26·IX·

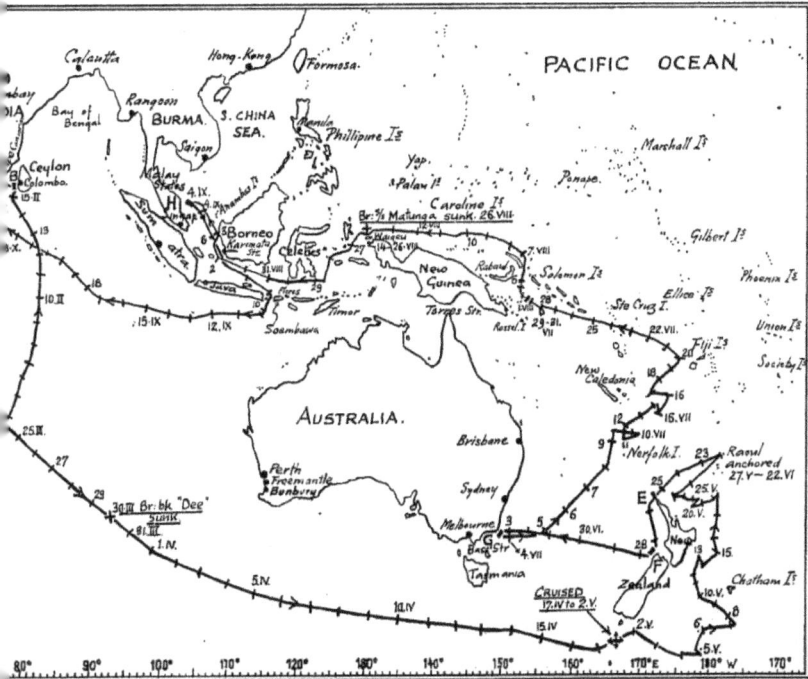

PLATE. XI.

REVIEW OF GERMAN RAIDING OPERATIONS. 1914-18.

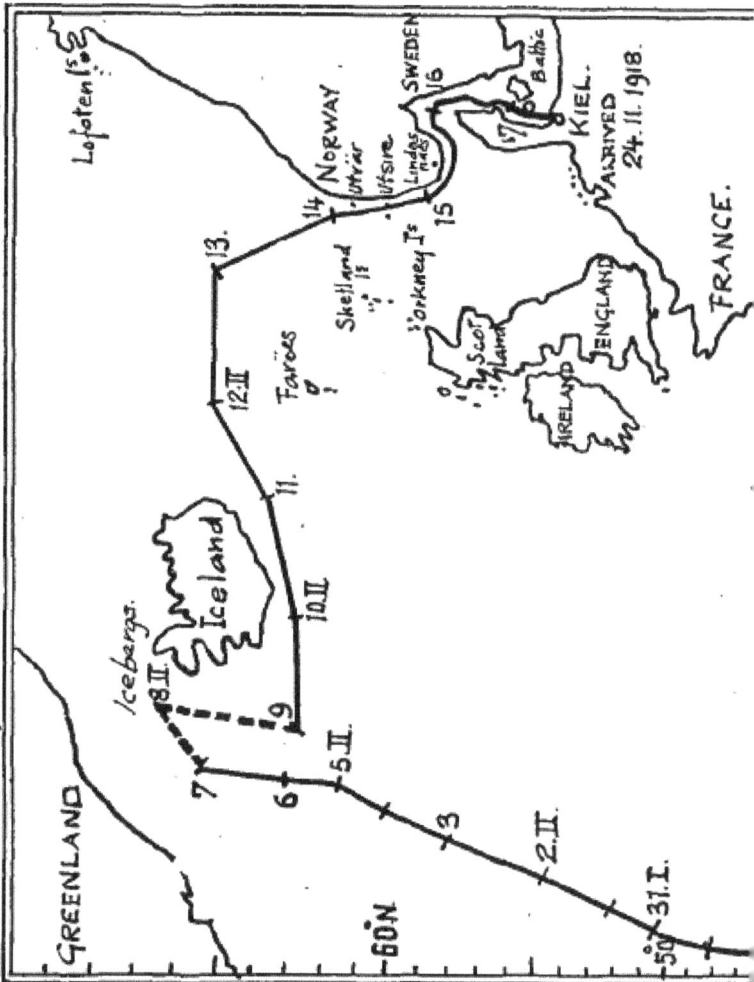

GREENLAND

Icebergs.

Iceland

Lofoten Is.

Faroes Is.

Shetland Is.

Orkney Is.

Scot Land

NORWAY

Jutria

Utsire

Lindes nas

SWEDEN

Baltic

KIEL.
ARRIVED
24.II.1918.

ENGLAND

IRELAND

FRANCE.

60°N

50°

31.I.

2.II.

3

5.II.

6

7

8.II.

9

10.II.

11.

12.II.

13.

14

15

16

17.

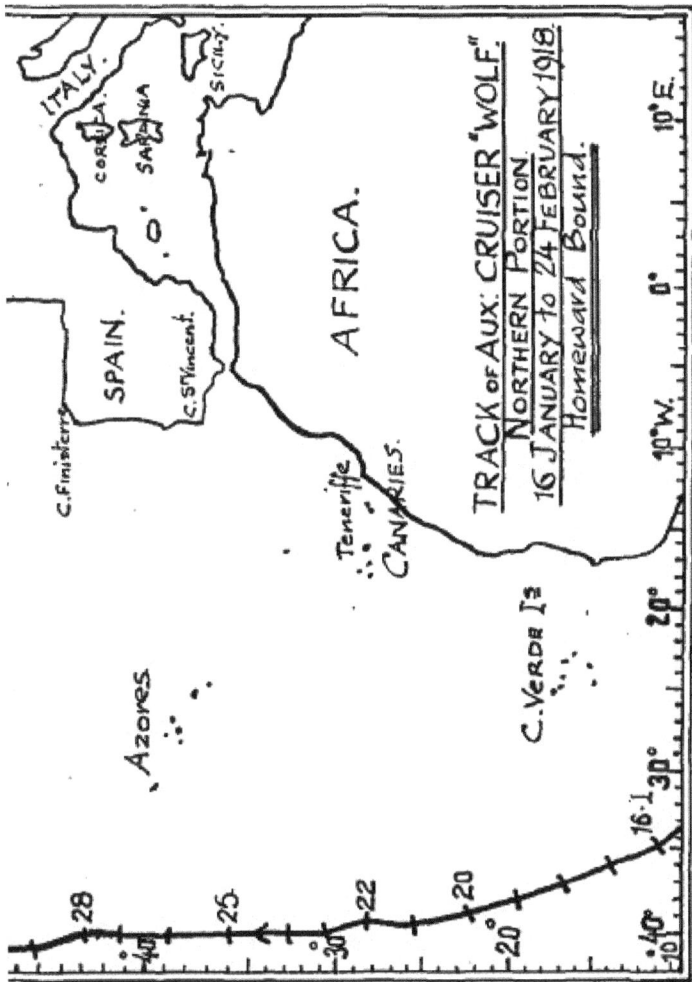

C.Finisterre

SPAIN.

ITALY.

CORSICA

SARDINIA

SICILY.

C.S. Vincent.

AFRICA.

Teneriffe

CANARIES.

Azores

C. VERDE Is.

TRACK of AUX: CRUISER "WOLF".
NORTHERN PORTION.
16 JANUARY to 24 FEBRUARY 1918.
Homeward Bound.

10° W.

0°

10° E.

28

25

22

20

20°

16·1·30°

40°

10°

30

Prepared by Naval Staff. (H/S). 1939.

(F9734) FOSH & CROSS L.TD

PLATE. XII.

O.U. 6334 (40)

REVIEW OF GERMAN RAIDING OPERATIONS 1914-18

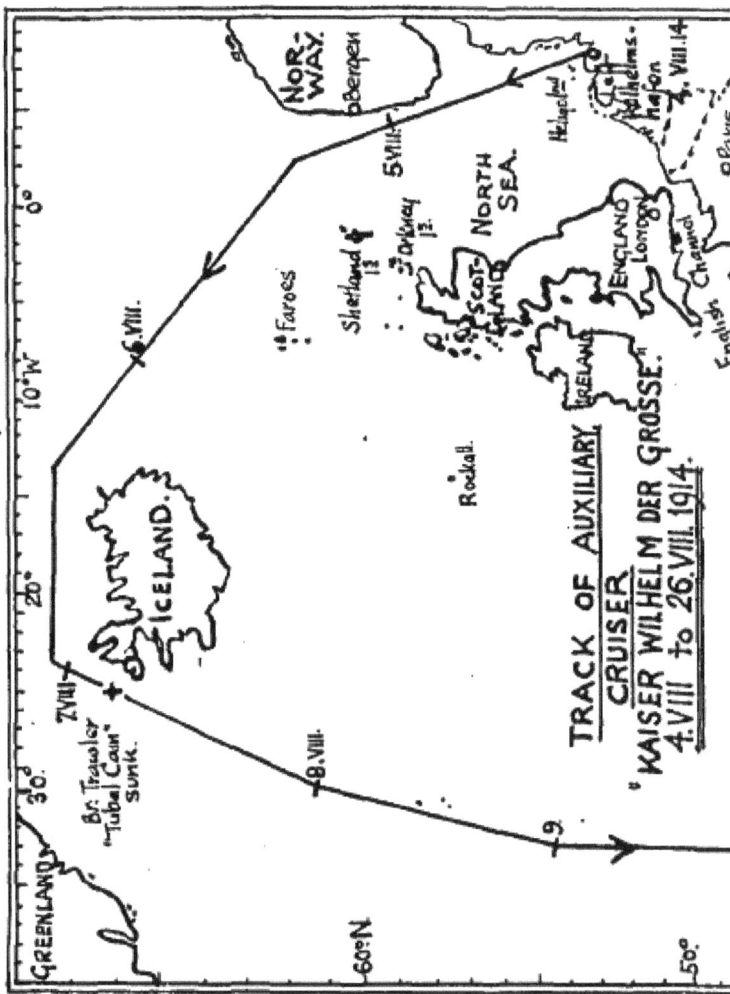

NOR-WAY.

Bergen

NORTH SEA.

Helgoland

Wilhelms-hafen

5.VIII.

6.VIII.

Faroes

Shetland 13

Orkney 13

SCOT-LAND

ENGLAND

London

English Channel

IRELAND

Rockall.

ICELAND.

Br. Trawler "Tubal Cain" Sunk.

7.VIII.

8.VIII.

9.

GREENLAND

TRACK OF AUXILIARY CRUISER
"KAISER WILHELM DER GROSSE."
4.VIII to 26.VIII. 1914.

30°

20°

10°W.

0°

60°N

50°

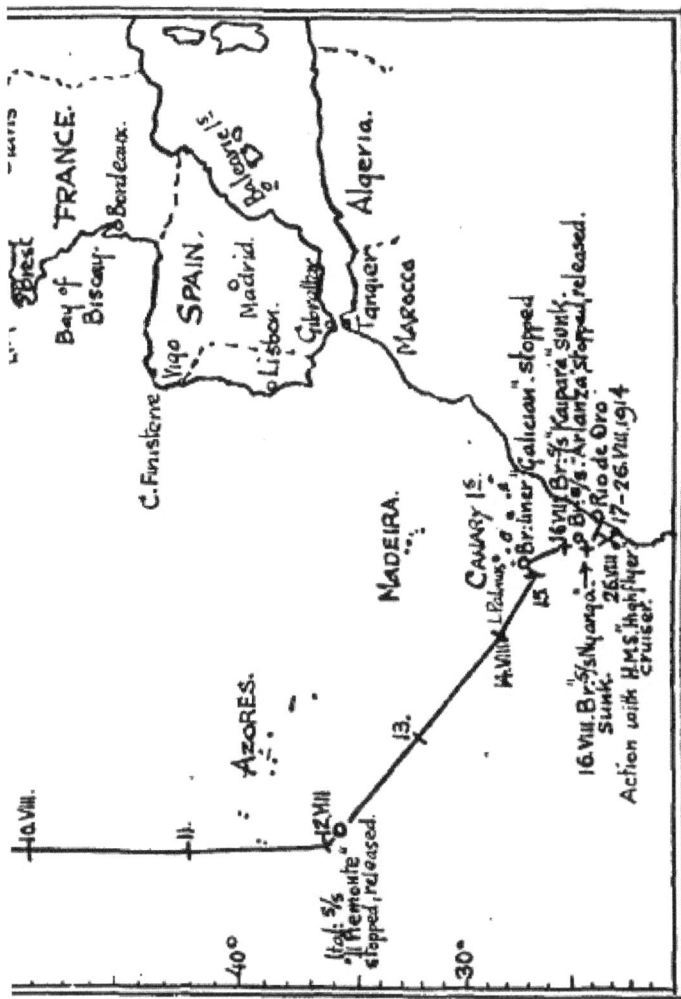

PLATE XIII.

O.U.633Y(40)

N.S. H/S. 1939.

(F.9734) FOSH & CROSS LTD.

BRAZIL.

PERNA

BOLIVIA.

BAHIA
4.IX.14.

PARAGUAY.

RIO DE JANEIRO

SANTOS

ARGENTINE

CAP TRAFALGAR
22-28.VIII.

URUGUAY
19-22.VIII.
"CAP TRAFALGAR MONTEVIDEO.
FROM
BUENOS AIRES.
18.VIII.1914.
RIO DE LA PLATA.

60°   50°   40°

N·S. H/S. 1940.   (F.9734) FOSH & CROSS L™

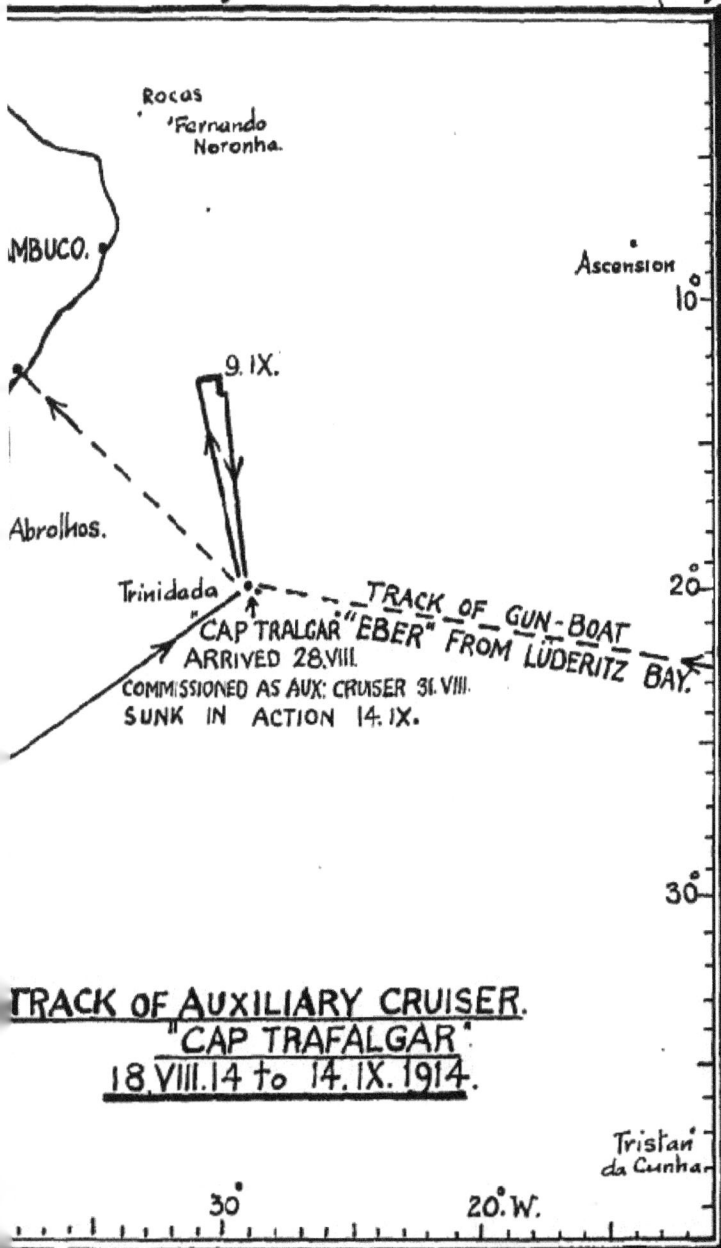

Rocas
·
Fernando
Noronha.

MBUCO. ·

Ascension ·
10°

9. IX.

Abrolhos.

Trinidada

TRACK OF GUN-BOAT
"CAP TRAFALGAR "EBER" FROM LÜDERITZ BAY.
ARRIVED 28.VIII.
COMMISSIONED AS AUX: CRUISER 31.VIII.
SUNK IN ACTION 14.IX.

20°

30°

TRACK OF AUXILIARY CRUISER.
"CAP TRAFALGAR"
18.VIII.14 to 14.IX.1914.

Tristan
da Cunha

30°   20°.W.

PLATE XIV.

1	9 Jan 1917	Br: S/s Gladys Royle	3268t	sunk.
2	10 " "	" " Lundy Island	3095	"
3	21 " "	Fr: Bk: Charles Gounod	2199	"
4	24 " "	Br: Schooner: Perce	364	"
5	3 Feb " "	Fr: Bk: Antonin	3071	"
6	9 " "	Ital S/v Buenos Ayres	1811	"
7	19 " "	Br: Bk: Pinmore	2431	"
8	26 " "	" " British Yeoman	1953	"
9	27 " "	Fr: " La Rochefoucauld	2200	"
10	5 Mar "	Fr: " Dupleix	2206	"
11	11 " "	Br: S/s Horngarth	3609	"
12	14 June "	U.S. schooner A.B. Johnson	529	"
13	18 " "	" " R.C. Slade	673	"
14	8 July "	" " Manila	731	"

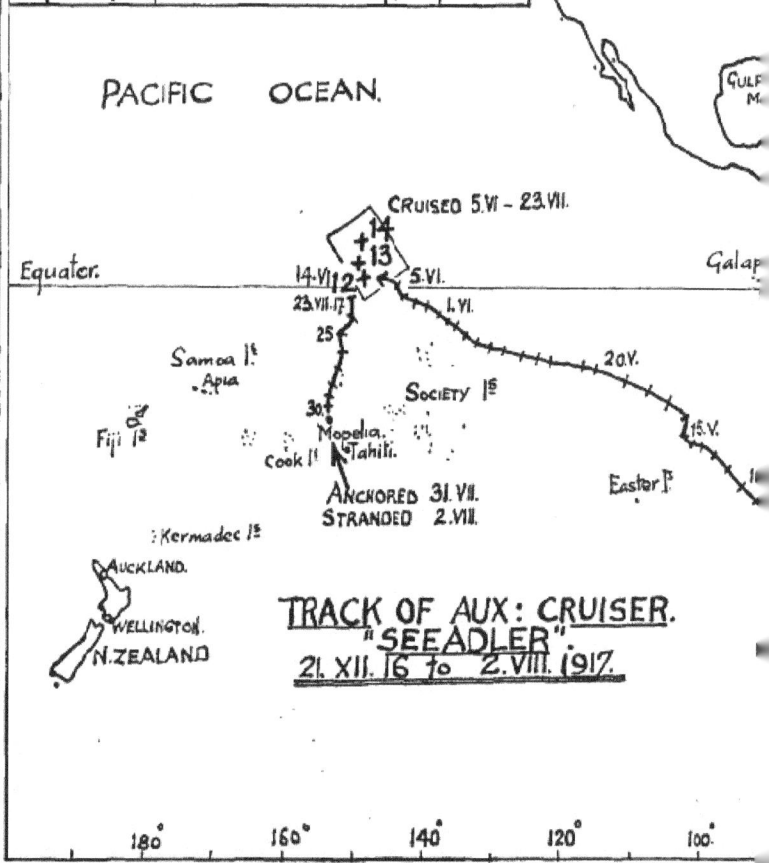

PACIFIC OCEAN.

NORTH AMERI

GULF
M

CRUISED 5.VI – 23.VII.

+14
+13

Equator.   Galap

14.VI 12 +   5.VI.
23.VII.17   I.VI.

25   20.V.

Samoa Iˢ.
. Apia   SOCIETY Iˢ

Fiji Iˢ   30

Mopelia.
Cook Iˢ Tahiti.   15.V.

ANCHORED 31.VII.   Easter I.
STRANDED 2.VIII.

: Kermadec Iˢ

AUCKLAND.

WELLINGTON.
N. ZEALAND

TRACK OF AUX: CRUISER.
"SEEADLER"
21. XII. 16 to 2. VIII. 1917.

| 180° | 160° | 140° | 120° | 100. |

GREENL^ND

ICELAND

25.XII.
24
26 Faroes
Shetland 23
18
22
60

1.I.17.

SAILED.
21.XII.1916.
PLYMOUTH FROM NORDER AUE.

EUROPE

:A.

ATLANTIC

AZORES
9.I +1
10.I +2
CANARY 1 ½

15.I
C.VERD 1 ½ AFRICA 20°

OF
XICO.

7 +5
+8
+3
9 +6
+10 CRUISED 21.I - 11.III. 0°
ago 1 ½ 4 +11
Fern +
Nor. 16.III.
14

S.AMERICA.

Callao
20.I.

21.III.

OCEAN. 20°

Antofagasta

Juan Fern
5.X Coquimbo.
Valparaiso Montevideo
Talcahuano B. Ayres.

5 1.IV.

Cape
Town
40°

Y.17.

Penas
Gulf
25.IV.
C.Horn. 15.IV.
20.IV.
18 60° 40° W 20° 10° 60°

25.

25

Falkl^ND 10.IV.
66 1 ½

PLATE XV.

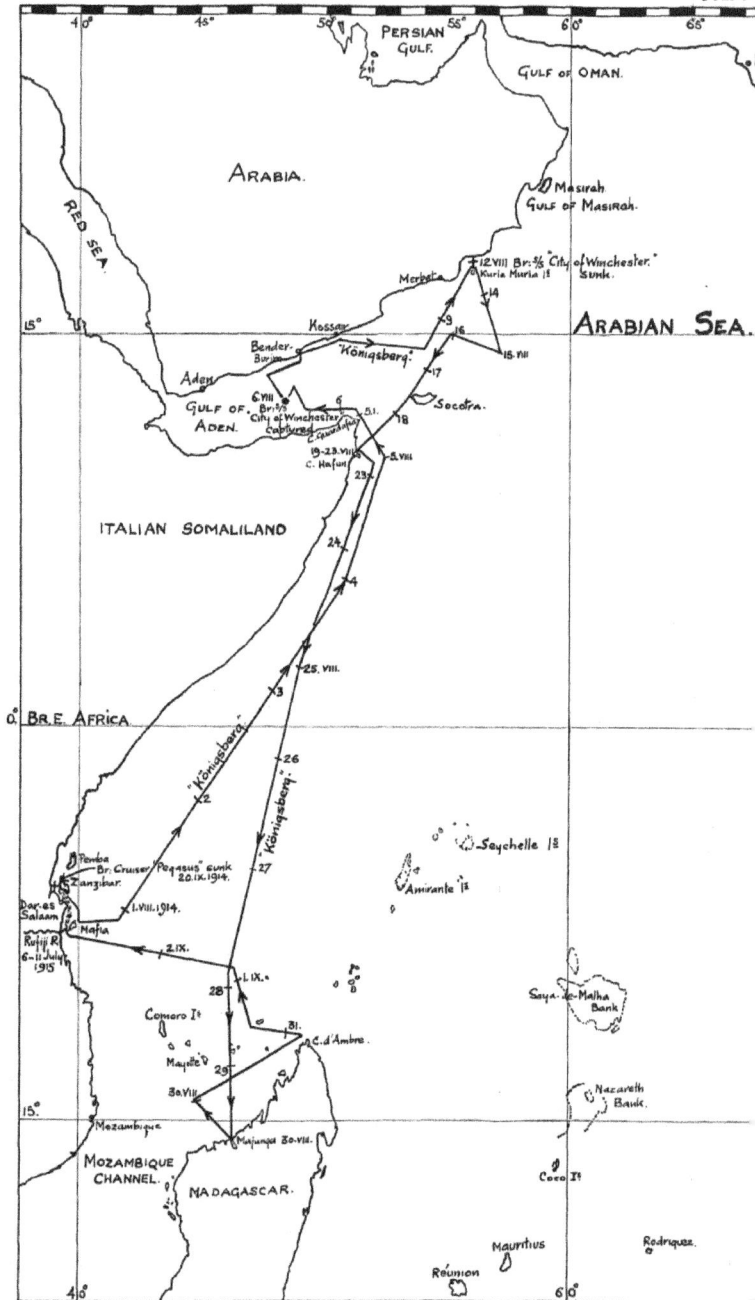

40° 45° 50° 55° 60° 65°

PERSIAN GULF

GULF OF OMAN.

ARABIA.

RED SEA

Masirah
GULF OF MASIRAH.

12.VIII Br. S/S "City of Winchester" Sunk.
Kuria Muria I.
Merbat
14
9
16
17
15.VIII

ARABIAN SEA.

15°

Kossar
Bender-Burya
"Königsberg"

Aden
GULF OF ADEN.
6.VIII Br.S/S City of Winchester Captured

Socotra.
5.I.
18
8.VIII
19-23.VIII C. Hafun
23
24
4

ITALIAN SOMALILAND

25.VIII
3

0° BR.E. AFRICA

26
"Königsberg"
2
"Königsberg"
27

Seychelle Is

Amirante Is

Pemba
Br. Cruiser "Pegasus" sunk 20.IX.1914.
Zanzibar
Dar-es-Salaam
Mafia
Rufiji R. 6-11 July 1915
1.VIII.1914.
2.IX.
28
1.IX.

Saya-de-Malha Bank

Comoro Is
31
C.d'Ambre
Mayotte I.
29
8a.VIII
Majunga 30.VII.

15°

Mozambique

Nazareth Bank.

Coco Is

MOZAMBIQUE CHANNEL.
NADAGASCAR.

Mauritius
Réunion
Rodriguez.

40° 60°

70° 75° 80° 85° 90° 95°

RACHI

INDIA

BOMBAY

CALCUTTA   CHITTAGONG

Ganges R.   BURMA

Black Pagoda   14.IX.

18.IX.   13.IX.

12.IX   12/13.IX

RANGOON

BAY of BENGAL

"Emden"

18.IX.
Gulf of Martaban

LACCADIVE Is.

MANGALORE   MADRAS
Bombarded 22.IX.

22   21   "Emden"   20   19

11.IX

ANDAMEN Is.

23

10.IX.
9.IX.

MERGUI ARCHIP.

9

8.X.

NICOBAR Is.   26.X. (Nank
Kachal Coaled
25X   Sombrero Channel
Gt. NICOBAR

C.Comorin

24.IX.

25/26   CEYLON
26   Colombo   25
25 IX

"Emden"   22   23.X.   24

30.X.

6

T.Iladum
Mali Atoll   27   22   19

16   16/16   18   19
18   19
19

MISICH 18

15   28

MALDIVE Is.

29-30 Coaled.
Felidu Atoll.

1.X.

Suadiva Atoll.

SIMALOER   Coaled 4-5

31.X.   NIAS

3.X.

2.X.

6°

"Emden"

3.X.

12x

Chagos Archipelago.

Diego Garcia
9-10.X. Coaled.

oaled 6-7.X.

Cocos Is.
8.XI.
9.XI A

MALA

2

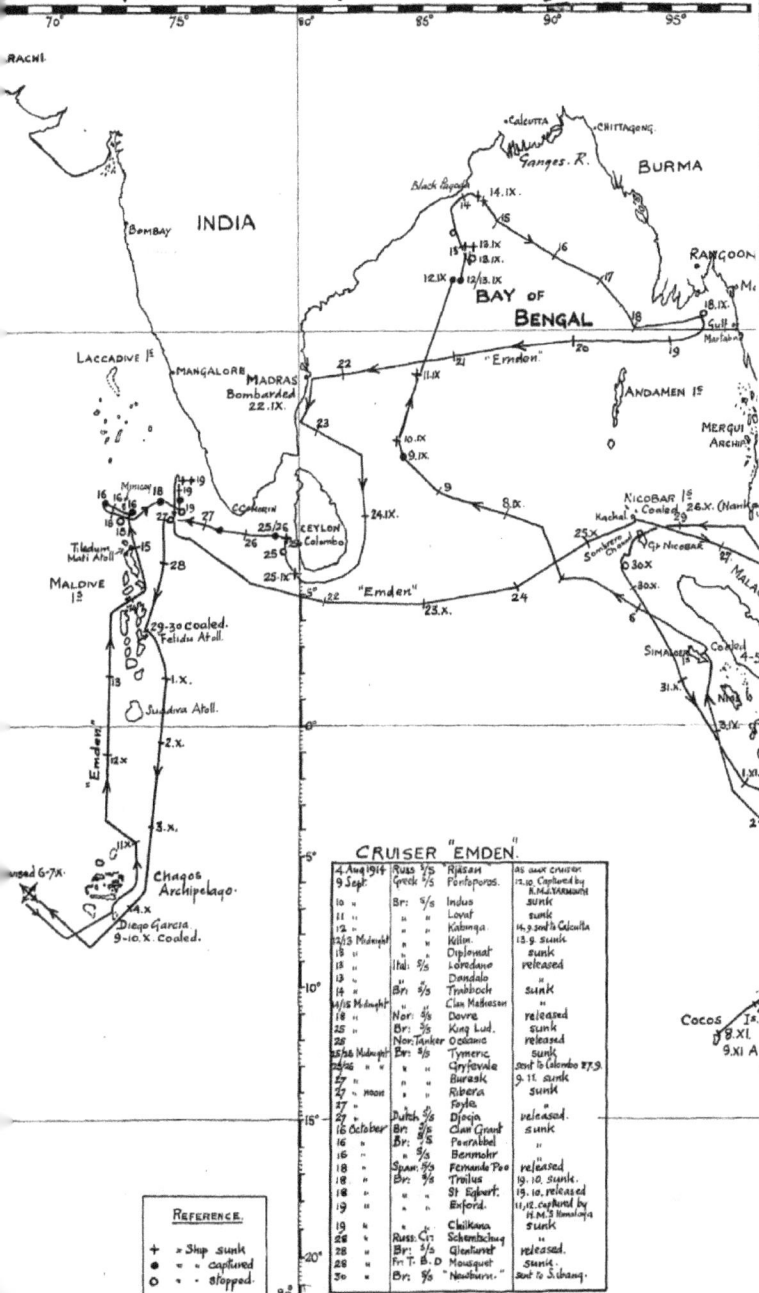

CRUISER "EMDEN."					
4 Aug 1914	Russ.	S/S	Rjasan		AS AUX CRUISER
9 Sept	Greek	S/S	Pontoporos.		12.10. Captured by R.M.S.YARMOUTH
10 "	Br.	S/S	Indus	sunk	
11 "	"	"	Lovat	sunk	
12 "	"	"	Kabinga	14.9 sent to Calcutta	
12/13 Midnight	"	"	Killin.	13.9 sunk	
13 "	"	"	Diplomat	sunk	
13 "	Ital.	S/S	Loredano	released	
13 "	"	"	Dandolo	"	
14 "	"	"	Trabboch	sunk	
14/15 Midnight	"	"	Clan Matheson	"	
18 "	Nor.	S/S	Dovre	released	
25 "	Br.	S/S	King Lud.	sunk	
25 "	Nor.Tanker		Ocama	released	
25/26 Midnight	Br.	S/S	Tymeric	sunk	
26/26 "	"	"	Gryfevale	sent to Colombo 27.9	
27 "	"	"	Buresk	9.11. sunk	
27 " noon	"	"	Ribera	sunk	
27 "	"	"	Foyle	"	
27 "	Dutch	S/S	Djocja	released.	
16 October	Br.	S/S	Clan Grant	sunk	
16 "	Br.	S/S	Ponrabbel	"	
16 "	"	S/S	Benmohr	"	
18 "	Span.	S/S	Fernanda Poo	released	
18 "	Br.	S/S	Troilus	19.10. sunk.	
18 "	"	"	St Egbert.	19.10. released	
19 "	"	"	Exford.	11.12.captured by H.M.S. Himalaya	
19 "	"	"	Chilkana	sunk	
26 "	Russ.Cr.		Schemtchug	sunk	
28 "	Br.	S/S	Glenturret	released	
28 "	Fr.T.B.D		Mousquet	sunk.	
30 "	Br.	S/S	"Newburn."	sent to S.abang.	

REFERENCE.

+ = Ship sunk
● = " captured
○ = " stopped

15°

20°

5°

10°

60°

LEONAUR

ALSO FROM LEONAUR
AVAILABLE IN SOFTCOVER OR HARDCOVER WITH DUST JACKET

THE FALL OF THE MOGHUL EMPIRE OF HINDUSTAN *by H. G. Keene*—By the beginning of the nineteenth century, as British and Indian armies under Lake and Wellesley dominated the scene, a little over half a century of conflict brought the Moghul Empire to its knees.

LADY SALE'S AFGHANISTAN *by Florentia Sale*—An Indomitable Victorian Lady's Account of the Retreat from Kabul During the First Afghan War.

THE CAMPAIGN OF MAGENTA AND SOLFERINO 1859 *by Harold Carmichael Wylly*—The Decisive Conflict for the Unification of Italy.

FRENCH'S CAVALRY CAMPAIGN *by J. G. Maydon*—A Special Correspondent's View of British Army Mounted Troops During the Boer War.

CAVALRY AT WATERLOO *by Sir Evelyn Wood*—British Mounted Troops During the Campaign of 1815.

THE SUBALTERN *by George Robert Gleig*—The Experiences of an Officer of the 85th Light Infantry During the Peninsular War.

NAPOLEON AT BAY, 1814 *by F. Loraine Petre*—The Campaigns to the Fall of the First Empire.

NAPOLEON AND THE CAMPAIGN OF 1806 *by Colonel Vachée*—The Napoleonic Method of Organisation and Command to the Battles of Jena & Auerstädt.

THE COMPLETE ADVENTURES IN THE CONNAUGHT RANGERS *by William Grattan*—The 88th Regiment during the Napoleonic Wars by a Serving Officer.

BUGLER AND OFFICER OF THE RIFLES *by William Green & Harry Smith*—With the 95th (Rifles) during the Peninsular & Waterloo Campaigns of the Napoleonic Wars.

NAPOLEONIC WAR STORIES *by Sir Arthur Quiller-Couch*—Tales of soldiers, spies, battles & sieges from the Peninsular & Waterloo campaingns.

CAPTAIN OF THE 95TH (RIFLES) *by Jonathan Leach*—An officer of Wellington's sharpshooters during the Peninsular, South of France and Waterloo campaigns of the Napoleonic wars.

RIFLEMAN COSTELLO *by Edward Costello*—The adventures of a soldier of the 95th (Rifles) in the Peninsular & Waterloo Campaigns of the Napoleonic wars.